RV Liv~~ing: Retire~~ into an RV with Social Security + RV Living for Senior Citizens

2-in-1 RV Living Compendium

Table of Contents

Book 1: Retire Into an RV with Social Security

Book 2: RV Living for Senior Citizens

Table of Contents

The Opportunity of Living the RV Lifestyle
Freedom, Ambition and Creativity Flourishes
RVing is quite affordable
To pay off debt and avoid it completely
The opportunity to share your life with others

A Brief Overview of Social Security
Who receives social security benefits?

How to Figure Out What Your Social Security Payments Should Be
Familiarize yourself with the calculation
Factor in your retirement age
Subtract Medicare premiums
Factor in income tax withholding

How to Figure out a Budget to live in an RV, based on Social Security Payments

Research and prepare your finances
Make your budget realistic
Initiate ways of saving
Ensure you earn money on the road
RV membership

How to Figure out if you can Live the RV Lifestyle or not

Enhanced closeness to your family members
Watch your money
Healthcare
Need to balance your life
Weather conditions
Loneliness

Chapter Two: How to Purchase an RV based on the Given Budget

Look for monthly payment options
Hunt for used RVs
Search online
Do not settle for a new RV
Customize later
Buy when dealers have offers

Desirable Specs in an RV

Length
Weight
Floor plan
Slide-outs
Height

More Factors to Consider When Obtaining an RV

Petrol or diesel

Have a goal
Plan for long trips and test trips

The Utilities to have in an RV

Solar panel
Tank dumping
RV plumbing

Towing your Vehicle

1. Flatbed trailer (also called an enclosed trailer)
2. A tow bar
3. Tow dolly

Realism about the Pros and Cons of Full-time RV Living

Pros
Full-time RVing is a permanent vacation
RV campgrounds and resorts are excellent places to stay
You see nature firsthand
Freedom to travel anywhere at anytime
Cons
You have no privacy
The pain of selling your house
Getting lost
You do not have neighbors

Chapter Four: What to do once you are on the Road

Handling Kids and Pets in an RV

Baby-proofing an RV
Bring along toys for entertainment
Always have a first aid kit
Do a headcount
Make frequent stops

Paid camp memberships
Boondocking
Different free camp land

How to Manage Yourself Financially on the Road

Set a travel budget
Recognize all your traveling expenses
Have a personal finance app
Put aside an emergency fund

Importance of an Emergency Fund

Surprise medical or dental expenses
Vehicle repairs
You do not make bad financial decisions
How to create one
Make cuts in your budget
Sell something
Make More Money

Health Insurance

Medical expenses are fully covered
Supplements a senior medical insurance
Covering pre-existing diseases
Tax benefits

What to do about Debts

Decrease expenses and Increase income
RV living to pay off debt is not terrible
Sacrifice is necessary
Work more, pay debts

Possible Avenues for Part-time Jobs and how to work Remotely while RVing

Adventure photography
Remote control race car driver
Resort, camp, or park employee

Towable RVs

Towing your Vehicle
4. Flatbed trailer (also called an enclosed trailer)
5. A tow bar
6. Tow dolly

New Vs. Used
Year and Quality
Negotiation Tips
Financial Considerations When Buying an RV

Additional Factors to Consider When Obtaining an RV
Petrol or diesel
Single vs. doubled windowpane
Extra points for Firsthand vs. secondhand RV

Chapter 2: How to Get Started Managing Yourself on the Road

Your Transition from Home to RV
Planning Phase
Convincing Your Significant Other
Leaving That Chapter of Your Life Behind
Budgeting For RV Living
Budgeting Apps

Importance of an Emergency Fund
Surprise medical or dental expenses
Vehicle repairs
You do not make bad financial decisions
How to create one
Make cuts in your budget
Sell something
Make More Money

Downsizing From Home to RV
Organizing
Items From Your House You Will Need

The Utilities to have in an RV
Decluttering
Selling, Donating and Disposing of Clutter

Choosing Your Domicile

The Best State to Register your RV

How to Receive Mail while Living in an RV
Use of mail forwarding services
Receiving mail through family or friends
Using mailboxes at UPS stores
Campground deliveries

When You Start on the Road Full-Time
RV Parks and Senior Campgrounds
Boondocking
Join Groups and Meet New People

Chapter 3: Healthcare and Insurance

Healthcare Options and Plans for RVing Seniors and Retirees
Medicare and Medigap Plans

Medicare Plans, Requirements, and Companies. Which is Best for You?
Medicare Medical Savings Account (MSA) Plan
Plan F
Plan G
High Deductible Plan F
Medical Savings Account Plan
Medicare Advantage Plan
Medigap Plans

Free Bonus for the Readers

As you go ahead and start your RVing journey, wouldn't it be amazing if you could share it with others and gain followers?

The best way to do this by far is by starting a YouTube channel. And I have a special bonus for you.

Get the 'YouTube Celebrity' video course for **FREE**. This course will take you step-by-step through making a successful YouTube channel and help you gain subscribers on YouTube.

All you have to do is go to this link, **http://eepurl.com/ggIwmD**, and enter your name and e-mail ID.

By signing up for the course you would also be signing up for my e-mail list, to which I send e-mails with bonus RV living tips and content.

Retire Into an RV with Social Security

How to use Social Security to live in a Recreational Vehicle (RV) Full Time

Introduction

Nowadays, many things motivate families and individuals to settle their lives on the road. Some may be running away from housing loans and debts, while others may be escaping from the recurring expenses of a permanent home. Even as some people engage in RVing for such questionable reasons, others see RVing as a settlement and beyond the conventional.

If you once hit the road for RVing on a short trip, it is not weird to try full-time RVing. Without a doubt, this kind of lifestyle will give you unexpected adventures and delights. You can go anywhere without leaving your family members. Carrying them around may be awesome as you will share the joy.

Most people hit the road with savings from their earnings. It may take time to save for full-time RVing, and therefore a majority goes on short trips. For people who are fortunate to get social security payments, full-time RVing may become a lifestyle.

Social security payments come as a lump sum that one can use for various expenses incurred while RVing full-time. For instance, accruing an RV as a first-time RVer may not be a hard endeavor. Moreover, sustaining yourself and family members you may be carrying along with you will be easy.

Even so, financial management skills may be required since you will survive with the social security payments all your life. You need to manage the cash flow, earn more and be in charge of your expenses. If your social security payment does not allow you to go full-time RVing, you may have to forfeit it for some time. Make more money and embark on your plan to go full-time RVing in a style you will enjoy.

This book is prepared to give you the right information needed for successful full-time RVing. With the advice herein, one will be able to make the best of full-time RVing with social security.

Chapter One: How to Live in an RV with Social Security

The Opportunity of Living the RV Lifestyle

The opportunity of living the RV lifestyle comes with a wild ride filled with amazing travels. AN RV life is going to make you appreciate so many things that you would not enjoy if you were living in your own house. AN RV lifestyle is not just for a specific group of people, as nowadays even students have embarked on this lifestyle. Below are things you need to know about the RV lifestyle.

Freedom, Ambition and Creativity Flourishes

RVing full-time is just a dream for many. As long as you are willing to take the right steps to achieve this dream, it will make you feel ambitious and motivated to explore more. When RVing, you will have an opportunity to meet new people every day unlike when you are in a typical home. You will view the world and see new parts of it.

RVing makes you more productive and energetic. When RVing, you will spend most of your time on the beach paddling, kitesurfing, swimming, strolling and viewing the ocean or sea. Such views you cannot experience from the comfort of your home.

RVing is quite affordable

Many people view owning an RV as very expensive. If you choose to live in an RV permanently, the only costs you will have is buying the RV. You can buy a decent RV at a very affordable price, and get lots of locations that offer free or accessible parking and camping.

AN RV will cost you relatively lower than buying a house. Owning an RV will ensure you don't pay rent if you do not hold a home yet. Living a regular life come with tougher financial times with a larger fraction of your income going to rent and utilities.

To pay off debt and avoid it completely

Living in an RV will help you settle and manage your debts. By selling your house and living in a recreational vehicle, you will cut on costs and save you money. Being debt-free comes with much freedom and makes you do what you love.

Some people have lost lots of property, and others are living with lower standards, or lost their jobs due to debt. A motor vehicle will reduce the risk of having to get a mortgage.

The opportunity to share your life with others

Many RVers work together in countries building homes, eradicating poverty, providing shelter, and empowering the young and old. While they are doing this, they also expand their lifestyle and enjoy their traveling lifestyle at the same time.

Being an RVer comes with full-time and part-time job opportunities. You may get jobs seasonally that will help you sort out a few of your bills. While you do this, there is still plenty of time left for you to explore and enjoy your RV.

You might not get all the answers about the RV lifestyle, but if you want to give it a trial, it can be a rewarding and exciting experience.

A Brief Overview of Social Security

Social security is a federal payment intended to protect people and their families from loss of earnings owing to retirement, disability or death. Social security is an essential section of the old age, survivors, and disability insurance programs managed by the social security administration. Since inception, social security has been a vital tool for promoting the wellbeing of those who can no longer work. This insurance and welfare plan pays benefits to retirees, workers who are disabled and survivors of deceased workers.

Who receives social security benefits?

Generally, a person must have worked for not less than ten years to receive social security retirement benefits. Nevertheless, the number of years to be eligible for disability benefits or benefits for surviving family members may be less than ten years.

The social security payment is one of the largest government programs in the world. It pays out hundreds ·of billions of dollars per year. Who gets all this money? Below are people who receive this:

Retired Workers

Over two-thirds of those who receive social security beneficiaries are retired workers. Fascinating statistics indicate that more than half of these numbers are men.

Disabled Workers

Disabled workers are also among the high number of beneficiaries getting social security payments. Nonetheless, the definition of social security is different as compared to other programs. Social security only pays out for when there is total disability. There are no benefits paid for partial disability or short-term disability.

Spouses

Spouses of the deceased or disabled workers can receive social security payments.

Children

Children of retired, disabled and deceased workers can receive social security payments; however, they need to be less than 18 years old.

How to Figure Out What Your Social Security Payments Should Be

Often, it can be difficult to anticipate how much you will receive from social security. If you have several years from retirement, it may be harder to predict the amount. Familiarizing yourself with how the authorities calculate your benefits can help you budget for retirement. Besides, this knowledge will help you boost your future social security payments. Here is how to estimate the amount you may get from social security in retirement.

Familiarize yourself with the calculation

The relevant authority calculates social security payments using the 35 highest earning years in your career. They then adjust the count for inflation. In the event that you have worked for more than 35 years, the authority leaves out your lowest earnings years from the estimate. As a result, this leads to a higher payment. People who have not worked for 35 years have zeros averaged into their social security payment calculation and get smaller payments.

For instance, workers who become eligible for social security payments can get their benefits by multiplying the first $895 indexed monthly earnings by 90%. Then, multiply the remaining earnings of up to $5,397 by 32% and incomes over $5,397 by 15%. The sum of these three values, rounded off to the nearest 10 cents, is the initial payment amount. Notably, the cost-of-living adjustments and delayed retirement credits can increase payments above this amount.

Factor in your retirement age

Your age when starting social security plays a critical role in your payment amount. It is imperative to note that your monthly social security payment reduces if you claim payment before retirement age. In most countries, the retirement age is between 66 and 70 depending on your birth year. You can boost monthly payments each month if you delay claiming between your full retirement age and 70 years.

Subtract Medicare premiums

If Medicare premiums are deducted from your social security plan, it may affect your payment. This year, the average Medicare premium is $134 per month. The law prohibits Medicare payments from decreasing social security payments for existing beneficiaries; therefore, a hike in Medicare premiums cannot be more than your annual social security cost-of-living adjustment.

Factor in income tax withholding

Many people pay income tax on their social security payments, particularly if they have other sources of retirement income. Nevertheless, if social security is the only source of income, you pay no tax on it. In case you have other sources of income such as a pension, part-time work, interest and dividends, then that income flows into the social security payment calculation formula. Consequently, you may have up to 22% of the social security payments withheld for income tax.

How to Figure out a Budget to live in an RV, based on Social Security Payments

Before embarking on an RV lifestyle, it is important to evaluate how economical it might turn out for you. Evaluate whether your social security earnings can support your RV lifestyle. Many people all over the world have dreams of living an RV life, but are not sure due to finances. Many RV potentials are unsure if they can afford the RV lifestyle, especially after their retirement.

Before spending your social security payments on an RV lifestyle, come up with a budget that will help you service your expenses. Below are ways to help you come up with a budget that will guide you to live an RV lifestyle with your social benefits.

Research and prepare your finances

Take your time to evaluate the RV lifestyle. Determine how much money you need to save to afford this lifestyle. Set up a budget, create and determine a plan for a monthly travel budget. Establish a current budget for your home as this will give you your spending habits. From this, it is easier to set up a budget for your RV living. Find ways of saving money while you are on the road and earn. Plan your RV lifestyle budget before you embark on it officially.

Make your budget realistic

Scrutinize your members and be honest with yourself. A dishonest RV lifestyle budget on paper will not serve your long-term goals. Prices of RVs may vary depending on the various options you have for analysis. Plan for your monthly budget to be sure on how much you are likely to spend monthly. Fixed expenses you are likely to incur include food, travel, entertainment, restaurants, laundry, health insurance, camping fees, and repairs.

Initiate ways of saving

To afford the RV lifestyle, you have to save seriously. The fact that some people spend too much on their RV lifestyle does not imply you also need to spend the same.

Live on a budget that is simple and affordable for your RV lifestyle. Limit buying things on impulse or making unbudgeted purchases. Before purchasing a gadget, confirm whether it is necessary.

Ensure you earn money on the road

To maintain a budget for your RV lifestyle, you can work while you travel. Most campgrounds and national parks have part-time jobs available. You can take advantage of these amenities and save yourself money during your stay.

RV membership

Having an RV membership will save you money with discounts at some RV resorts, with some travel insurance companies, for taking tours, and attending rallies etc. Go for a budget that works for you effectively. You should have no problem living and enjoying an RV lifestyle when you have sorted out a budget. By carefully planning and knowing your limitations, there is no reason for you not to enjoy an RV lifestyle of your choice. Choices will depend on how much money you are willing to spend, places you want to visit and the adventure you want to experience. With a working budget, your dream of living an RV lifestyle can be a dream come true.

How to Figure out if you can Live the RV Lifestyle or not

Before you choose whether you can live a regular life or an RV lifestyle, there are many factors to put into consideration. You need to know what it takes to succeed. The RV lifestyle is tasty but is it worth it for you?

Here are factors to consider before engaging in an RV lifestyle:

Enhanced closeness to your family members

How much are you attached to your loved ones? Do you like to spend time with your loved ones or spouse? If you love your family enough to be with them all the time, an RV lifestyle would suit you. Leaving your loved ones when you are deeply connected to them will give you emotional distress, and that is why a regular life will be perfect for you.

Watch your money

You need unlimited cash to live a full-time RV

lifestyle. You have to consider all the costs that come along with this lifestyle. The most significant costs are fuel and food. Regardless of how wealthy you may think you are, make sure to keep a tight check of the budget as you might end up bankrupt.

If you have doubts about your financial stabilities, then consider living a regular life unless there is a turnaround of events in the future.

Healthcare

If you want to live an RV lifestyle with health issues, this may bring more harm to your health than good. There are not many plans that will help you get all the care you need in RV living. If you need to get regular check-ups or even medication from a pharmacy, then RV living will turn out to be a big challenge for you. If you cannot do without a prescription, then consider living a regular life.

Need to balance your life

If you are employed, the RV lifestyle is not your thing. Those who work online will also find it hard to do the work that needs to be done. The temptation to keep enjoying your surroundings might hinder you from achieving your career goals. If you know you cannot work on a schedule outside an office, then you should reconsider living a regular life.

Weather conditions

Sometimes the weather may not be favorable the moment you want to start living an RV lifestyle. You might find the weather too cold, and you might not have a generator to keep you warm and comfortable in your new place. When you want to live somewhere, be sure to consider the weather conditions of that place. If you are going to avoid all these things, then you have no option than to consider a regular life.

Loneliness

Staying without a social life is hard for almost everyone. If you are never happy being alone and enjoying your own time, then an RV lifestyle might not be perfect for you. You might try RV living to fight loneliness and finally stop when you realize it is not something you enjoy. If you are the type of person who enjoys other people's company, consider living a regular life. Now it is time to come out and do what you think is right for you. You never know your journey until you try it yourself.

Chapter Two: How to Purchase an RV based on the Given Budget

Your budget plays a considerable role in the process of purchasing the best RV. AN RV can cost you tens of thousands of dollars. It is essential to stick to your budget to avoid unnecessary financial drawbacks. You need the best negotiating and buying strategies to secure the optimal RV. Below are a few factors to consider when purchasing an RV based on a given budget:

Look for monthly payment options

Some dealers will offer monthly payment options. This method of payment may not be the best, especially with retired people who may not have a source of income per month. When you take the option, take care of the monthly payments based on your monthly budget.

Hunt for used RVs

Unless you have permanently fixed your mind on purchasing one, make it a goal to find a well-maintained used RV. You will save a lot of money. With a well-cared used RV, you may only need very little to update some components.

Search online

Go online and search for the best RV sellers that are offering in the online market. You can get better prices from private owners than from dealers and brokers. Owners may give you the history of the vehicle and that is a huge factor in decision-making.

Do not settle for a new RV

When purchasing an RV based on a given budget, it is wise to avoid new ones. Buying used RVs allows you to have more control over your budget. It also gives you a chance to do more customizations and improvements. Spending less will spare you some money that you can use to have more fun with your loved ones.

Customize later

It is imperative to think long-term when budgeting for an RV. Please do not be afraid to obtain a simple model and upgrade it later. Modifications to fit the desired interior can be done down the line. Think of an RV like a home that requires ongoing improvements.

Buy when dealers have offers

RV dealers operate on monthly and yearly schedules when they give offers. You may find sweet spots during the middle of fall when the RV season is ending. At this time, most RV dealers give away their vehicles at reduced prices.

Desirable Specs in an RV

What kind of RV should one buy? Sometimes, this is a hard question to answer since it depends on a person's discretion. Well, there are a few things that one should consider when choosing an RV. Below are some important factors to put in mind when selecting an RV:

Length

The length of an RV is a restraining factor for RVers. Plenty of roads prohibit specific lengths of vehicles. Even though lengthy RVs may have more space that facilitates mobility, be on the lookout not to get fines on the road.

Weight

Weight should be a vital factor to consider when planning to purchase an RV. Just as some roads restrict the height of vehicles, they also inhibit weight; thus, it is wise to take a close look at the capacity of the RV.

Floor plan

Bear in mind the must-haves in your RV before selecting the best fit for your full-time RVing. Choose the RV with the amount of space you want. For instance, you may need an oven, bathroom or sleeping space for at least three people. Only an RV that conforms to the floor plan that is enough for you and your family is the right fit for you.

Slide-outs

Slide-outs are attractive features to check when purchasing an RV. The slides are sections of the RV that slide out when parking to increase living space. If you prefer a more open RV, selecting an RV with opposing slides would prove helpful.

Height

Even though low clearances are rare, you need to watch out the height of the RV you are obtaining. It is prudent to notice the low clearance signs on the road if you want to keep your roof.

More to this, there are numerous factors to consider when picking an RV. It is true that obtaining an RV is a mix of extreme excitement and a lot of stress in making the right decision; therefore, it is good practice to let your preference prevail.

More Factors to Consider When Obtaining an RV

Petrol or diesel

There are many advantages to purchasing an RV with a diesel engine. Diesel engines are famous for their robust nature. The engines have more power that translates to more torque, and this implies a better towing capacity and stronger uphill acceleration.

Also, diesel engines can handle a more intense, long-distance type of driving than a petrol engine. This means that a diesel engine will handle the workload better if you are using your RV full-time and moving a lot.

Nevertheless, cold weather can cause problems for diesel engines. Because of the more complex engine, you cannot take a diesel to a regular mechanic for repairs. You will require a diesel mechanic, and this may be more costly to maintain and repair.

Single vs. doubled windowpane

Some people think that replacing single-paned windows on an RV may result in a lasting insulation quality. This is not the truth since double-paned windows have a limitation that makes them impractical for use in RVs. The double-paned windows tend to fog up when subjected to strong vibrations.

Double-paned windows are not designed for use in high-vibration surroundings. If your RV does not come with standard double-paned windows, it may not be cost-effective switching them out. Moreover, if you have a travel trailer, you might want to stay away from double-paned windows altogether.

Firsthand vs. secondhand RV

Pros of buying a firsthand RV

- You get a brand new vehicle – top of the line RV off the manufacturer's assembly line.

- Full manufacturer warranty takes effect the moment you make the purchase.

- You do not have to worry about damage or wear and tear issues when driving off for the first trip.

- You can get the exact features you want for the amount you have.

Cons of buying a firsthand RV

- It can be expensive depending on the features present.

- One may incur more expenses in the future because the manufacturer does not customize all RVs.

- Insurance premiums for a new RV will be higher.

Pros of buying a secondhand RV

- A buyer may save a significant amount of money as compared to buying a new RV.

- One can opt to rebuild, redecorate and restore the RV to personal preference.

- Insurance premiums are lower for a secondhand RV.

- A buyer can take time to customize, repair, and upgrade existing components.

Cons of buying a secondhand RV

- Most sellers may not disclose what might be wrong with the RV.

- You may not know how depreciated the RV is in value.

- Often, the manufacturer's warranty has expired.

- One may spend a considerable amount of money on upgrades.

Note: It is cost-effective to buy a used RV when starting.

The Best State to Register your RV

When you fail to do your research concerning the best state to register your RV in, the whole process may be a difficult situation. The first requirement is declaring a state as your primary residence. It would be best if you tried to find a state that has its taxation system set up to your advantage.

Without a doubt, you have eliminated all except the following nine states:

- Tennessee

- Texas

- Washington

- Wyoming

- Alaska

- Florida

- Nevada

- New Hampshire

- South Dakota

Even though Tennessee and New Hampshire do not have an income state, they tax interest income and dividends; therefore, we can leave them off the friendly list.

Generally, you have to pass through the state occasionally to renew your vehicle registration, and driver's license. This makes Alaska off the list of the states above. The state is tax-friendly, but making an annual pilgrimage that far north may be extreme for some people.

Having struck off Alaska, Tennessee and New Hampshire from the list, we are down to six friendly possibilities. Concerning sales tax, there is not much difference between the remaining six states.

The personal property tax will affect the

process of RV possessions. Which states have personal property tax? Among the remaining six states, Florida and Washington have a personal property tax; thus, we drop two more out of the list of full-time RV-friendly states.

Therefore, the final four possibilities are:

- Nevada

- South Dakota

- Texas

- Wyoming

Chapter Three: How to Transition from Stationary to RV Living Full-time

Emotional Aspects of an RV Lifestyle that Rarely Gets Discussed

What is the RV lifestyle anyway? It can mean different things to different people. It may refer to vacations, camping trips, full-service tailgating or a seasonal home for the snowbird. AN RV lifestyle, in short, is what you want to have.

AN RV lifestyle can be a dream for everyone, but it is also a massive adjustment since it can be transformational. At some point, you will find this very overwhelming and sometimes be unable to prepare for the emotional challenges that will come with RV living.

Below are some of the emotional challenges you will face with an RV lifestyle:

Leaving your family and friends
The first few months will be difficult for you,

especially if you have a close relationship with your family and friends. You will have one or two panics, although you will still have fun. Your feelings about leaving them will solely depend on how often you see each other, and how much you rely on each other for support.

Some will be happy for you and others will make you have second thoughts about your decision. They cannot understand why you would want to choose a lifestyle that is entirely different from theirs.

Leaving them should not stress you much since, in recent times, there are so many media platforms to keep you connected to the people you love. Communicating with your loved ones often will let them know you are thinking about them.

No matter how tough this experience may turn out, focus on the reasons why you chose your RV lifestyle.

Selling your properties

You will be excited but, at the same time sad that you will be letting go stuff that you valued. It will be hard for you leaving a home you lived in for the most extended times of your life. The experience will be awful for you with intense emotions, but remember to focus on the bigger picture of why you made that choice.

Losing your traditional identity

There are not many emotions here but fear. You might have been a co-worker, church member or a manager. The roles and routines have changed and maybe your identity. It can be hard to start thinking about why you chose an RV lifestyle in the first place. The only thing to keep you going in such a situation is to follow your heart and keep your mind open. Make sure all the decisions you take only bring happiness and fulfillment to your life.

Fear of losing conveniences and community

You may be more connected to your loved ones, but the sadness may come when you realize the importance of your community. It is a time that you are alone, and you will not be around people anymore. Loneliness becomes a reality in your life. With time, you will realize how familiar you are with your area, and how entrenched you are to your community. You need to communicate early with those that matter in your community.

Everyone reacts differently in the transition to an RV lifestyle. Be prepared for ups and downs in this journey. The good news is that most RV emotions will fade away as soon as you start to enjoy your trip.

What to leave behind and what to take when you transition

It's not possible for you to take everything that you have in your home, into an R.V. It is best to get rid of clutter and give away most of the memorabilia to your friends and family.

Given below are some tips that can help you to properly organize and declutter your possessions, before you transition into living in an RV and also after. Feel free to adopt whatever tips that you like.

Take out these items

Old shoes

Shoes often don't age well and you are not doing yourself a favor by wearing them or keeping them in your house. Get rid of them.

Clothes you've almost never worn/cannot fit into anymore

Have you kept any clothes that you dislike or don't wear very often? It is probably time to let go of them. If you have clothing you can't fit into anymore, then save yourself some space and do away with them as well.

Books you have never read

If you purchased a book about 12 months ago and still haven't read it, chances are that you might never do so. In this scenario it is better to discard as you can only have a few select items that you can keep.

Expired products including medication

These items should at no cost be used (especially medication). Systematically group expired items into a trash bag and send them on their way out.

Previous year diaries/calendars

If you didn't use it last year, chances are you won't use it ever, especially with the brand new diary or calendar that you have now got.

Clear up dry and broken pens

We all have pens that are empty, broken or those that we dislike. We never use them and so one should get rid of them.

Clear out junk drawers

Junk drawers full of un-needed items like

rubber bands, old batteries, wires and chargers of gadgets that no longer work.

Ugly decorations

Decorations that you feel do not look good should be taken out.

Do it with the seasons

Seasonally declutter your house, at the change of every season.

Buy less stuff

It's simple. Resist the urge to add to your clutter by buying things that you don't need. If it has a function, try and discard something else from your possessions.

Kitchen

Odd spices

Out with all the old funky spices that you kept for cooking a special recipe!

Keep the pans that you use

Only 2- 3 pans are used daily, if you make a certain dish which requires a certain utensil or gadget every year (like for July 4th or the Super Bowl) you can keep that utensil. The rest you need to discard.

Give every item a home

Have an assigned place for each category of dishes/ingredients/cutlery/gadgets in your kitchen in a planned layout. That way you will have an idea as to where to keep a certain item.

Return the items to their place

Once you are done using something return it to its assigned location immediately, so that you are left with one less thing to do in the end.

Keep the countertops clean

Always avoid crowding out the countertops as you only have limited space. Return items you won't need any further back to their respective places.

Clean right after you finish

Once you are done with cooking make sure that the kitchen is clean so that when you come back next time you won't have to clean it.

Don't let your sink fall into chaos

The sink might be an anchor for your kitchen, littering it can lead to litter in the kitchen and vice versa.

Paperwork

Legal Documents

Any legal documents should be kept.

Tax-related documents

All documents that could be filed for tax returns should be kept.

Evaluate your subscriptions

Take a careful look at your magazine and newspaper subscriptions as well as newsletters that you receive, if you don't read the magazines then it's time to cancel your subscription.

Digitizing your memories

Digitize photos and documents

You can scan your old photos and documents to form digital copies. Digital copies can be stored in a small yet powerful hard drive.

Digitize movies and music

CDs/DVDs can take up whole shelf loads of space. Try the alternative. And next time you're tempted to buy a physical copy of any of these items, opt for the digital one instead and use the physical copies as the last resort. Seriously, music streaming is the future now anyway.

Turn books into e-books

Many e-book facilities are out there, like Kindle, that let you read anywhere and you are free from having a physical copy with you. Plus once you have bought it you have access to it forever, in case you want to read it again, so you don't have to worry about losing your book.

Note

The tips given above come from a book named, *Clutter: Living Life And Leaving The Rest* by Stotra Anubhav. If you would like to know more about decluttering to transition into an R.V. home, then you can buy the book at **https://amzn.to/2E1Uxp5**. I highly recommend it.

How to Set Up a Recreational Vehicle

A recreational vehicle refers to a utility vehicle or trailer that has living facilities designed for temporary accommodation.

Every RV beginner needs to know the essential things they need to look for before they start traveling. For those who are new to camping trips, here is a step-by-step method of setting up your recreational vehicle.

The first thing is to arrive at an RV campground

Ensure your campground is free from all distractions like towed cars. Check in and inquire if there any discounts available for RVs.

Get a map for your campground and locate where your camping site is.

Observe the location given to you, and if your vehicle is too large, consider walking to the camp or using a different car. Know whether the place has enough space for you and all the facilities that you need for camping.

Know your RV

Learn how the RV operates if you are a first timer. In case of accidents, you will be in a position to fix them. It will save you a lot of time and money you would spend on a mechanic.

When you are familiar with your recreational vehicle, you are likely not to make an operational error.

For example, you have got no idea how many

amps your main breaker can hold, so you are likely to blow it. Such errors are avoidable by knowing your rig.

Ask for help

When setting up a recreational vehicle, do not fear to ask for help. You are navigating an expensive machine and being afraid of asking about it could be dangerous.

In most campgrounds you will find a campground host who will assist you in setting up your camp. If your camping area does not offer this, you can hire one or even ask other RVers. It would be a great way of making camping friends, and you can end up spending more time with them during your spree.

Carry stuff that you will need

You can consider stocking a tool kit with spare parts and add things your RV might need. For example, you might need extra fuses, light bulbs, nuts, bolts, connectors, and cables.

You are likely to watch television or need a refrigerator; hence, you will have to plug into your RV. You will need tools to plug in all these gadgets.

Level your ground

The ground may not always be flat on your campground; there may be a need to level it to ensure utilities work correctly. Consider taking a ride or a small trip to have a real experience of hitting the road for a long trip. Remove stones around your camping site or any protrusions. Fill in all small depressions and pack them tightly. Check the camp for low-hanging branches and obstacles lying on the ground.

RVing is a great way to travel and enjoy staying outdoors. Knowing the basics of setting up your recreational vehicle will reduce stress during your trip and make it more enthusiastic.

How to Receive Mail while Living in an RV

How do you survive when you are on the road without a physical fixed home address? It is never that complicated receiving your mail while still RVing.

You will never realize how important a mail delivery is, until when you are living away from home. Mail sent to your home address is delivered to your doorstep, and the only task is to pick them up. What happens to your letters when you choose an RV lifestyle?

Below, we discuss ways you can receive your mail while living in an RV:

Use of mail forwarding services

An RVer lifestyle comes with a lot of freedom because no-one wants to keep waiting for his or her mail for a long time. There are popular companies that offer mail-forwarding services. In most cases, the help you get a home address. Even so, the companies also offer the services to people who live as fulltime RVers. They deliver mails to the park where one may be camping. This is possible because most RV parks ask for your address. This way, mails delivered to the park can be sorted out to respective mail addresses.

Pick a provider that you trust to give you services that fit your RV. Comprehend the pros and cons of each method you are about to choose. You can always call your service provider to inform you what is in your mail at a small cost.

Receiving mail through family or friends

Many RVers use family and loved ones to receive their mail. All you need to do is to ensure whoever is forwarding the mail to you is organized and efficiently delivers the mail to you on time.

When RVing and on a tight budget, using family to receive mail will be a great way of saving on costs. The disadvantage with this method is in case many letters come every day, as it might be a bit difficult to forward them.

Your mail might also be mishandled and delayed. It is advisable to have your email repackaged into one parcel and forwarded. While in an RV, you will need to maintain clear communication with your family so they know the exact location to send your mail to.

Using mailboxes at UPS stores

UPS stores offer a full package of business and communication services including shipping, packing and delivery services. UPS is something to consider when selecting a solution for your RV lifestyle since they offer personal packages and handle mail carefully.

With UPS, you generally find a post office near a place you would like your mail delivered to. The challenge with this method is that it is expensive and not recognized as a legal address.

Campground deliveries

Many inventions have come up, for example, Amazon Prime for RVers. They usually have mail delivered to RV parks with two days shipping guaranteed. If your other options for mail deliveries cannot work for you, consider trying out this one.

All you need is to let the service providers know where your campground is and they will call you once your mail is delivered.

Getting mail on the road may not be as difficult as many think.

Full-time Living in an RV

Many people tend to think that RV living is just for retired travelers; however, there are many reasons to live in an RV full-time irrespective of age or job status. It is an excellent experience for those who do not want to spend top dollar on a permanent home. In the modern world, RVing has become a standard way of living. RV living requires a particular approach and mindset to make it feel like home. Below are things you should do to prepare to live in an RV full-time.

Select the right RV

Having the right RV is essential, especially when you are planning on RVing full-time. It would be a huge leap to assume that you already have the best RV when planning to live in an RV full-time. Some RVs are made to be for short trips; therefore, if you get one meant for short trips, it will not work well for full-time living. Even if spacious and elegant RVs may be expensive to buy, they prove to be the best for full-time RVing. Make full-time living worthwhile with the best RV there is out there.

Come up with a realistic budget

While transitioning to the new lifestyle, it is prudent to be mindful of your budget. It would be best if you struck a balance between the income, savings, and spending. As a retiree, one must be keen to create a budget that concurs to his social security payment received. Over-indulgence will only drain the bank account faster than you anticipate. This may be unfortunate and may end your full-time living sooner than desired; therefore, cutting costs and living by what you can afford is very important. In reference to the point above, it is wise to obtain an RV that has the lowest cost in terms of insurance, fuel, and maintenance.

Have a goal

The most straightforward approach to plan for the future in full-time RVing is to think about why you are doing it. Perhaps you want to enjoy your social security payment with family. On the contrary, you may want to quench your adventurous nature. Having a goal justifying your full-time RVing affects many decisions including the type of RV you get and how you budget. For instance, aimless traveling may have a drastic impact on your gas spending. Being in a place for an extended period may result in an increment of what you spend on camping fees. Whatever the reason, let it be a good and planned endeavor. Always keep the reason for choosing a full-time RV lifestyle in mind.

Plan for long trips and test trips

Full-time RVing means that you will be on the road for most of your time. As a good practice, you will want to consider making several short trips before making long trips. This prepares your mind concerning what long trips may turn to be. For instance, long trips require adjusting how you gather supplies. Taking a short trip will enable you to estimate the volume of supplies you may need for long trips. In short, short test trips will help you realize how much you enjoy the lifestyle of full-time RVing.

You will want to do some footwork to ensure you are making the right decision before embarking on full-time RVing.

The Utilities to have in an RV

It is prudent to keep your RV stocked with basic supplies, non-perishable foods, linens, and clothes. This way, you will be ready to go anywhere at any time.

It is true that everyone has favorites and must-haves they cannot survive without while RVing; however, below is a list of some stock items to keep at all times while on board:

- Dishes/cooking utensils

- Pots and pans

- Heavy-duty extension cords

- Insect repellent

- Plastic bags (large and small)

- Road flares

- Rope and bungee cords

- Shovel (small folding type)
- Sports equipment
- Adapters for 30 amp and 50 amp outlets
- Batteries
- Binoculars
- Bottle/can opener
- Camera and memory cards
- Soap and toiletries
- Sunscreen
- Jacket/raincoat
- Maps and GPS
- RV toilet paper
- Matches/lighter
- Nature field guides
- Pillows, blankets, sheets
- Picnic basket
- Firewood

- First-aid supplies

- Flashlights, lanterns

- Folding chairs

- Games

- Grill and fuel

- Toolkit

- Towels

- Trash bags

- Umbrellas

- Water hose (white potable water type)

Before you hit the road, ensure you balance your load and avoid over-packing. Keep in mind the weight label on your RV.

In addition to the list above, it would be in order to have the following utilities in the RV:

Solar panel

When you are driving or camping, sunlight pours down on the roof of the RV. Based on the budget you are running with, you can obtain a solar panel. The panel may be a small 5-watt panel that keeps the battery charged.

Alternatively, the panel can be a 900 watts panel that gives you the freedom to run lights, refrigerators, fans, and electronics anywhere the sun shines.

Tank dumping

RVs are equipped with toilet facilities and a sewage holding tank. This part collects the waste in a toilet. An ideal RV should always have this to ensure that you can relieve yourself while onboard. Ensure you have the connector pipe that drains the contents of the tank to a dump station.

RV plumbing

It is incredibly important to understand the RV plumbing system and the RV plumbing parts to include. At first, the system that delivers water in an RV may seem complicated. The system comprises of a water pump and a water heater. There are RV plumbing fixtures and plumbing fittings that you should use. This should not turn out to be problematic because most RVs are already fitted with the necessary plumbing parts.

Towing your Vehicle

It is cautious to invest in a towing solution that works for your RV and vehicle. A majority of

RV owners overlook the need of having a towing solution. They think that an RV should not necessarily tow anything. There are three primary approaches to tow a car behind an RV.

1. Flatbed trailer (also called an enclosed trailer)

A flatbed or enclosed trailer facilitates one of the easiest ways to tow your vehicle behind larger RVs. This method offers a larger space to bring a car, off-road vehicles, or even bring in more storage to your existing RV. The flatbed or enclosed trailer provides full support for your vehicle, including its brake and light system; however, investing in a flatbed or enclosed trailer will be more expensive.

2. A tow bar

A tow bar gives you the chance to tow a vehicle behind your RV while keeping all four wheels on the road. Notably, this is one of the most common and affordable methods to tow a vehicle behind an RV. In this method, safety chains and cables are used to offer stability between the tow bar and vehicle. For safety purposes, you will need to invest in a supplemental brake system or lights. The system alerts those on the road when you turn and brake. It is critical to ensure that you can tow safely with a tow bar before investing in this solution.

3. Tow dolly

A tow dolly tows a vehicle by placing the rear wheels on the road and the front wheels on the dolly. This is meant for those who may not want to invest in an enclosed or flatbed trailer and do not want to tow using a tow bar. Nowadays, some tow dollies come with surge or electric brakes. In addition, some even come with lights, and you may not need an additional system to notify other drivers to know if you turn or brake.

It is crucial to carry out some research to determine the best fit for your towing needs. Furthermore, let your choice of towing solution align to your budget.

Realism about the Pros and Cons of Full-time RV Living

The RV lifestyle comes with a wild ride filled with amazing travels. An RVer is going to appreciate so many things once taken for granted when living in a permanent house. AN RV lifestyle comes with terrific moments. On the other hand, at times, struggles and frustrations of full-time RVing may make you miss the comfort of your home. Below are the pros and cons you need to know about the RV lifestyle:

Pros

Full-time RVing is a permanent vacation

The idea of traveling around the country may seem like an endless road trip of fun. It can be a permanent vacation when you are retired or enjoying your social security payment. Learning to adjust and live as a full-time RVer may be hard in the beginning, and one may take time to get into the flow of this lifestyle. When you get used to the lifestyle, it feels like you are on vacation and enjoying your time.

RV campgrounds and resorts are excellent places to stay

Many full-time RVers can ascertain that RV campgrounds are lovely places to stay for at least a whole day. The campgrounds are clean, quiet and have beautiful natural sceneries. Because of this, many campsites are perfect places for full-time camping. On the other hand, some campgrounds may be untidy and crowded and living there may not augur well with many people.

You see nature firsthand

As a full-time RVer, you can park somewhere amazing with beautiful natural scenes. You will see sights that you would not have noticed if you opt to stay at home. Traveling across the country will give you a new appreciation of unusual, unique and stunning places. There are many incredible national parks and tourist attraction sites that people are yet to experience. Living on the road implies that you have the opportunity to see whatever you desire and stay as long as you want.

Freedom to travel anywhere at anytime

One of the greatest things about full-time RVing is the freedom it offers. If you do not like where you are camping, you can move on to the next place. On the contrary, if you love where you are camping, you have the liberty of staying there for another day, week or a month. In case you abruptly change your mind and want to go to the next camping site, all you need to do is hit the road. The freedom to travel where the wind takes you is a unique thing to this lifestyle. It can be addictive yet fascinating.

Cons

You have no privacy

In the recreational vehicle and camping sites, there is entirely no privacy. Most times, you will have people camping next to your RV. It can be stressful, especially at a time you want to be alone. You will always have to keep your voices down and avoid yelling since your neighbor can hear you. You will have to share bathrooms and a small living space with people accompanying you while traveling. For example, if you have kids, you can never hide to do private things. They will always locate where you are.

The pain of selling your house

Sometimes when starting an RV lifestyle, the lifestyle compels you to sell your house to buy a quality motorhome. You will have to take money from the house sale and put it in a bank to finance your RV. After all, there will be a part of your mind that will convince you that you do not need the house. Before you sell your home, know the worth of the RV you want to purchase. The finances required may be a fraction of your social security amount. The value depends on the make, model and year of manufacture. It might pain you to sell your home and property, especially when you have called it home for years. You are likely to experience intense emotions. Remember, even if you are RVing full-time, you will need a place to call home.

Getting lost

When starting your RV lifestyle, it is not going to be the same as your permanent home. At times, you will have to go out to get groceries or even hang out for enjoyment. The area is new to you, and you have no idea of where shops and other amenities are. You find yourself lost, especially in your new place, unlike your permanent house where you knew all the routes. In your hometown, you could drive all the places you need to go; however, in an RV you might be afraid since you are not familiar with the surrounding areas.

You do not have neighbors

When you are planning to get into the RV lifestyle on a full-time basis, you will have to realize that you are tying yourself to isolation. Well, there are rare instances when you meet new friends at campgrounds. Often, it will just be you and your family alone. Being in isolation for too long is not advisable. It may lead to psychological issues, such as anxiety and depression. To maneuver this problem, one should visit destinations that allow them to mingle with others.

Notably, the RV lifestyle comes with its advantages and disadvantages. Sometimes, you might not get the difference between the regular and RV lifestyles; however, when you experience the two lifestyles, you can choose what fits your life best.

Chapter Four: What to do once you are on the Road

Handling Kids and Pets in an RV

RVing has always been an exciting activity for a family. It is one of the highly rated ways to increase family bonds and create lasting memories. It can be an utterly fascinating activity if done frequently. As a person who wants to enjoy the social security payment, full-time RVing will bring Heaven down for you. It is no wonder one may introduce the world of RVing to their little ones, not forgetting pets. Kids and pets will require special attention when RVing and this is the reason this part aims to educate you about handling them in an RV. Below are tips for managing both kids and pets onboard an RV:

Baby-proofing an RV

Exceptional care needs to occur when securing a child when RVing, either on short trips or long trips. If you use a towable, you are less likely to change the car seat options. Nevertheless, you need to be more careful with your child in a motorhome. In an RV, you need to set up a secure area where the baby can sleep and explore when accompanying you on your RV adventures. Baby-proofing is a cautious way to make the RV cabins a friendly and safe environment for a young one.

Bring along toys for entertainment

Kids need things to keep them busy while you are traveling. Besides, pets also need some toys to play with as you hit the road. Most models have television screens that will be perfect for watching entertainment. Alternatively, you can obtain a handheld gaming system for your kids. This can keep kids from quarreling as you concentrate on the road. Bring all the toys for your kids and pets so they feel included in the journey. As a result, they will not complain about long trips.

Always have a first aid kit

Having an RV safety kit is good practice. The safety kit should include all first aid tools to attend to any emergency treatment effectively. Painkillers are also essential components of a first aid kit. It is also wise to bring along flares, at least one spare tire, flashlights and anything you need in the event of a vehicle breakdown. Ask your vet about the best pet medicines to keep in your first aid kit while you are on the road.

Do a headcount

As a rule of thumb, do a double check that you account for everyone before pulling up your stakes and start rolling out. Kids and pets may find their way beneath the RV when you stop. It can be easy to injure them if they cannot get out of the way in time. A pet may be taking a nap in the shade outside the RV while you make a stop and it may be easy to leave them. Check that everyone is inside the vehicle before setting out.

Make frequent stops

Even your pet cannot hold their bladder all day; therefore, rest stops every four hours or so will give them a chance to get a little exercise. The stops will also be useful for kids to stretch their legs, as well as keeping the driver from getting road fatigue.

Paid camp memberships

A paid camp membership is a private campground or RV park open only to members. Members pay a one-time membership fee and annual dues to gain access to the campground at any time. Paid camp memberships are cost-effective. Members only pay once, and, for registration and service, an annual membership. In addition, paid camps have all the amenities that may be costly outside the camp. The camps offer rental accommodation and spaces for tent camping.

Boondocking

Boondocking is the practice of pulling off the highway to stay at free locations in your RV. Notably, the spots where you park may have zero or limited facilities. For this reason, it is also called 'dry camping.' At times, boondocking means a rural area of rough countryside filled with dense brush. Some people still park at shopping mall car parks and truck stops. Experienced boondockers exercise caution while staying in such areas. You may stay for a night or two and have the discipline to avoid owners throwing you out. While boondocking, avoid downtown areas. You might be hassled, particularly in streets covered in beer bottles or near nightclubs.

Different free camp land

Usually, the authorities allow free camping in most US national forests and grasslands, unless otherwise marked. Even so, each national forest has slightly different rules. In some places, there are no fire restrictions, while you can only have a fire if you obtain a fire permit in some areas. It is therefore prudent to check the rules ahead of time to avoid trouble or unnecessary expenses. Generally, you are allowed to camp anywhere outside established recreation areas and developed campgrounds.

Note that you have many options when camping in a national forest. You may locate a nice pullover, and backpack into the woods to set up camp. On the other hand, you can find an attractive spot along a forest service road. This will require you to be self-sufficient because there will be zero amenities. For instance, there will be no picnic table, trash, or restrooms.

How to Manage Yourself Financially on the Road

Thousands of people never sit down to make a plan for their budgets, especially when traveling. Financial management is something not taught in many schools, but it is something we all need to deal with in our lives.

When traveling, you have a big task of managing your money; hence, you need to plan and execute your money during your traveling spree. You will have to set a budget, save and manage your money while on the road.

Below we have explained some tips to help you manage your finances when traveling:

Set a travel budget

Create a budget if you haven't already done so for your traveling. Figure out how much you need to spend on the road. Creating and sticking to your budget will be tough at first, but it pays off at the end. Your budget will wholly depend on your income.

Budgeting will help you see how much you are likely to spend on the road, and it will help you manage your money. Define your ideal travels and put on it a general price tag. Along the way, you may decide to change, but as long as you have money, you can keep up with all the plans that come your way.

Recognize all your traveling expenses

Many people do not know how much they spend on monthly total travel expenses. The idea is to have a track of all your traveling expenses accounted for to come up with a total amount. It would help if you also considered removing all unnecessary costs during your travel.

Doing this allows you to have a clear picture of how you spend while on the road, and how to manage your finances going forward. During your travels, make sure you take all receipts and balance them with your bank statements. By doing this, you will not find yourself running out of funds while traveling.

Have a personal finance app

Using this application will show you ways of managing money and budgeting for it during your travels. For example, tools like Quicken for Windows or Free Money Strands will allow you to consolidate safely, and manage and control your money in one place while on the road.

Using Money Strands means you are in a position to access your account balances, all financial transactions, your spending habits and budgets while traveling. Install this application anytime you are about to move as it will help you make smarter decisions and achieve your financial goals while still going.

Put aside an emergency fund

Stuff can happen while on are on the road. You can be caught up by a natural disaster or even an accident. You will have no option than to go back to your wallet whether you like it or not. For these instances, having an emergency fund will cover any emergency that comes your way when traveling.

Knowledge is power. If you follow the above tips, be sure to manage your cash the right way while traveling. Being able to manage your finances will make your travel exciting and fun.

Importance of an Emergency Fund

An emergency fund is some money set aside for quick and impromptu access to cover unforeseen problems. In other words, it is money that a person may earmark for expenses that come up unexpectedly. An emergency fund should be separate from retirement savings or a savings account that you may have for a specific purpose. When you start building an emergency fund, the hope is that you will never use the money; however, it will be there when you inevitably need to. Below is why you need to have an emergency fund when RVing full-time:

Surprise medical or dental expenses

Sometimes, one may get sick due to changes of weather. It is worse when you have kids and pets on board, and they develop all sorts of ailments. This kind of medical emergency requires you to have some money.

Vehicle repairs

You do not anticipate having vehicle breakdowns while on the road. Breakdowns happen at any time, especially when one least expects it. This may require you to have some money to contact the nearest gas station for repairs. Additionally, you may need some money to have a sleepover at the nearest inn if the RV breakdown is in the middle of nowhere.

It helps keep your stress levels down.

It is true that life threatens our financial wellbeing and causes stress when we face an emergency. If you do not have some money set aside for emergencies, stress will be a part of your life. Staying prepared with an emergency fund makes one confident that tackling the life's unexpected events will be easy.

You do not make bad financial decisions

Having some money to attend to your emergencies helps you avoid borrowing. Even though there are various ways one can quickly access credit, the interest accrued may not be favorable. Avoiding interest on debts and maybe penalties may be best for you.

How to create one

Make cuts in your budget

Scrutinize your budget and make several cuts, especially on unnecessary expenses. While on the road, cut down any impulse purchases and ensure you buy personal effects, groceries and other foods in bulk. Within a short time, the results could raise some eyebrows.

Sell something

Do not rush to sell your home! You probably have more options than your house. Look around the house and you will be amazed to find items not in use worth the right amount. For instance, you may find old toys, exercise equipment, an old piece of furniture and many more items. You can sell such things to raise an emergency fund before you hit the road.

Make More Money

There are many opportunities to do some quick work and earn a measurable amount. Working online is one of the common ways of raising money for full-time RVers. As you work, focus on building an emergency fund.

Health Insurance

Health insurance is a form of insurance coverage that pays for medical and surgical expenses incurred by the insured. The plan can compensate the insured for expenses incurred for any medical services or pay the care provider directly. Health insurance is often included in the employer benefit packages as a means of enticing and motivating quality employees. It is important for senior citizens to have health insurance.

The following is an explanation of the benefits of health insurance, especially to senior citizens:

Medical expenses are fully covered

You do not use your resources to get treatment when on any health insurance. As stated above, one gets compensated or medical expenses paid by the health insurance plan. Consequently, one saves the resources for other day-to-day expenses.

Supplements a senior medical insurance

One can pair private health insurance coverage with Medicare. This is a perfect way to ensure that a senior has sufficient coverage because Medicare has some limitations. An independent insurance agent comes in handy to help you understand any exclusion on a policy to avoid gaps in medical coverage.

Covering pre-existing diseases

Pre-existing ailments or diseases are symptoms, diagnosed illnesses or any existing or past health condition that exists at the time of applying for health insurance. The elderly are more prone to ailment attacks. Health insurance covers pre-existing diseases, and this is an excellent way to deal with ailments in senior citizens.

Tax benefits

The government avails tax benefits for people with health insurance. People who pay health insurance premiums qualify for tax relief. Senior citizens may get tax relief on social security payments that are subject to taxation.

It is a personal duty to be in charge of your health and start saving and investing in suitable health insurance in advance. At old age, health insurance will prove helpful to yourself and to your family members in a time of medical care.

What to do about Debts

The idea of selling most of your high-value possessions to clear your debts is terrifying; therefore, it is necessary to get a better alternative to get your debt settled.

Decrease expenses and Increase income

Some financial experts may mislead you into thinking that you can only build wealth and get rid of debts by increasing your income. While that is a great idea, dealing with your debts may largely depend on expenses than on income. Even with a small income, reducing expenses will help in managing debts.

RV living to pay off debt is not terrible

RVing can prove to be a great way to reduce expenses. Your property expenses, such as rent, water, and electricity bills will be none of your worries. This way, you can save and get the chance to clear your debts.

Sacrifice is necessary

While RVing, you will learn how to forfeit some expenses. Full-time RVing means that one would have to make a severe adjustment to expenses. Forfeiting some unnecessary expenses helps one to achieve a goal of becoming consumer debt-free.

Work more, pay debts

While RVing, you still have the opportunity of working remotely and earning. You can make savings from the earnings to help you gain a debt-free status.

Possible Avenues for Part-time Jobs and how to work Remotely while RVing

The concern of many people embarking on an RV lifestyle is whether they will afford RVing full-time. It is an enormous risk, especially when you do not feel sure about your finances.

Do you know you can fund your travel by getting a part-time job when RVing? It is effortless to sustain your livelihood while still on the road. Below is a list of part-time jobs you can do while working remotely:

Adventure photography

When you know about photography, and this is maybe one of your hobbies, start earning from it. Perhaps you even have a studio, and you can take advantage of your skills while RVing by selling your prints online.

Go to campgrounds and take photos, especially when there are events taking place. From this, you might find yourself becoming one of the best traveling photographers. You will be in a position to make money and, at the same time, enjoy your RV.

Remote control race car driver

When still RVing, you may offer to be a race car driver and make income from it. During an RV car-racing event, you can provide services like a remote control car racetrack, changing tires, racing simulators or even a diesel motorhome if you have some.

Providing these services is going to make you an incredible income that will help you maintain your RV lifestyle.

Resort, camp, or park employee

In most resorts and parks, part-time jobs for people who own RVs are available. Being a seasonal employee is excellent because it will help you make an extra coin to cater for your expenses while traveling.

Jobs can range from being a park ranger, housekeeper, lifeguard, front desk staff and ground keepers. There is a list of sites where you can access part-time jobs available for RV users, for example, Cool Works and Workers on Wheeled.

Become a travel blogger

You can make money by sharing your adventures and recommendations. You can also choose to write about beauty, fitness, popular culture, travel, and parenting. If your blogs get good traffic, then be sure to earn from it and continue enjoying RVing.

As you progress, you may even collaborate with a few sponsors to write and recommend their services.

Online tutor

If you have a computer and access to the Internet, tutors are on demand. Many students want to learn about different things' hence, you can do this while still RVing. You can tutor and teach online classes in a virtual environment.

Depending on where you are working from, there are great tools to connect you with students direct from your RV, for example, Tutor ME and ESL tutor, do not require you to have a teaching certificate. The schedule is flexible; hence, you can work virtually anywhere in the world and make money from it.

Before you get a job when you are RVing, get to understand what you want and need and do research on it. First, know your skills and ensure the work excites you. Then, choose a job that you feel entirely fits you.

The RV jobs might not make you wealthy, but at least you will be happy as long as you have no debts coming your way.

The Ability as an RVer to Tailor Expenses to Match Revenue

The RV life does not have to be that expensive. Many people associate an RVer as a very wealthy person who might not be the case. Perhaps this mentality was brought by the magazines and online photos we see phrasing an RV lifestyle as very expensive.

To afford to become a full RVer, you need to find out how to tailor your expenses to match your revenue.

Below are tips to help an RVer balance their expenses to match their income:

Choose the right RV

Choose an RV that perfectly fits your budget and plan. You can consider hiring an RV inspector to help you identify the different RVs available. Research adversely on this to ensure you make the right choice. To keep your bills low, avoid staying in one place for over a month, since you will start paying bills like electricity bills.

It will be quite expensive for you to choose an RV and then decide to change it after a while. You will have additional savings if you want an RV that best suits your income.

How to finance your RV

You may not have cash lying around to enable you to buy an RV. You might be forced to borrow from a bank or a credit union that specializes in RV loans if you plan on living in your RV.

Try to find a balance between your RV expenses and your income by finding an effective way to decrease your monthly costs.

Be on the lookout for free parking and camping

Joining an RV club will come with parking and camping discounts. There are even RV clubs that offer members places to stay; hence, cutting back on expenses and help you maintain your RV lifestyle.

Consider boondocking on public lands, or volunteer to work where you stay to receive a low-cost RV site.

Getting tax breaks

With the RV lifestyle, you have a choice to choose the place you call home. It will be cost-effective for an RVer to select a no-income tax state. Some states come with tax benefits; hence, consider living in one if you want to maintain an RV lifestyle. These states have no income, and that is why they are tax-free.

Tax breaks allow you to adjust on your spending and lets you live on any budget.

Get an RVer job

When you start traveling, it does not necessarily mean you have to stop working. Some RV parks hire full- time or even part-time RVers to handle and maintain parks. It will help you earn an allowance to cover other expenses in the month like electricity bills and food.

You can park your RV with other RVers for free, or even at a meager cost. These entrepreneurial opportunities will help you balance your expenses and revenue.

Are you an RVer, or are you just wondering how to do it? Follow the tips above to help you tailor your expenses and revenue at the same time.

Cost-saving Ways to make your Income last while RVing

When starting an RV living, your spending habits and budget are going to change.

There are ways to save money on RV life costs which will help lower your costs and make your RVing lifestyle more affordable and achievable. It is easy to ignore your expenses, especially when going on vacation.

Here we are going to discuss simple tips that will help you save money while RVing:

Have a plan and take advantage of free RV spots

Do enough planning to avoid yourself getting caught short without a place to stay. Get a place where you can get affordable services like accommodation and food. You can also consider getting a place where you can cook your food.

When RVing, find spots to park for free since applications are available to help you spot some. During your stay, you will save parking fees which will help save on costs.

Get a budget

Many people believe only people with money

can afford the RV lifestyle. What you need to do is to stay on top of your budget and live within your means. Without a budget, it's close to impossible to afford an RV Lifestyle.

Make a track of all your expenses while RVing as this is going to save on your income, and stop you from wasting money.

Register for RV memberships

The RV world has many memberships that will help you save money on various RV activities. By joining a group, you will have an opportunity to have discounted RV parking and campground fees.

Check out Good Sam and Escapees that offer good discounts on social networks. You want to save on costs and maintain your income while RVing, so consider joining the RV clubs.

Take an adventure in boondocking

Boondocking involves camping without hook-ups. It will save you lots of your hard earned money. Apart from saving on your costs, boondocking will offer you some beautiful camping locations. Most camping sites are free; hence, it will help you save on costs big time.

Try to stay longer in one camping site for as long as you can because this will give you a significant saving and cut down on your costs.

Time your vacations

If you want to save on costs during your RVing, time your vacations carefully. Consider traveling in a season that draws a lower number of tourists. During this time, prices are lower for almost everything; hence, you will get a good deal. Avoid traveling to favorite places during their busy seasons since the costs might be on the higher side.

Consider also RVing when the weather is favorable for you, and looking for an RV place with special events. You will save on money that you would have spent to make your RVing lifestyle comfortable in unfavorable weather.

It will be a great feeling when you are RVing and spend relatively little money. Follow the tips above and be sure to save, and make your income last while RVing.

How to Manage Data so you can keep Working

While working online, managing your data helps you to keep on going for as long as you want to work. You can create a hotspot with a mobile device or carry a portable Wi-Fi router when RVing. Below are tips on how to manage data so you can keep working:

Have a data plan

Being on a data plan has better value than paying as you use. On a pay-as-you-go basis, you pay per MB for data usage. With a data plan, your costs are fixed unless you go beyond your data allowance. This may be possible when you have either a mobile device or a Wi-Fi router.

Save data

You can save data by turning off maps, navigation, and location-based services. Besides, you can close applications on your mobile devices and computer when not in use. Switching off these applications may help you reduce data expenses. Put off your data connectivity on all devices when you are not using them.

Close background apps

Some mobile-based applications like Instant Messaging, YouTube and social media apps sometimes use background data. Ensure you completely close all background applications to save data. It is also a viable option to uninstall any applications that you are no longer using.

Set data alerts and limits

While using a mobile device as a hotspot, you can check and change your data usage settings. This way, you can be able to keep track of your usage. It also allows one to set custom alarms when you exceed a certain amount of data in a month.

You may notice more ways to manage your data. These are only a few tips to help you get an idea on how to save your data. Avoid incurring huge data expenses!

RESOURCES

https://thervnomads.com

https://rv-roadtrips.thefuntimesguide.com

https://gorving.com

https://wandrlymagazine.com

https://www.moneycrashers.com

https://rainyadventures.com

RV Living for Senior Citizens

How to Start and Manage Full-Time RV Living as a Retiree Over the age of 60

George Lee

Introduction

After working hard all those years, you finally retired. The last few years, you and your significant other have discussed taking your retirement years on the road. But now that the day has come when you can finally achieve this, you're wondering how to start and if you'll be able to financially support the full-time RV living lifestyle.

Whether you're retired and ready to take on your nomadic dreams or facing financial hardship and wonder if RV living is the way to go, this book is for you. This book aims to be a guide to help you start the new chapter in your life of full-time RV living.

If you're worried about being alone in this lifestyle, have no fear. There are thousands of senior citizens who started this chapter in their lives.

Some start by taking shorts trips because they want to test the waters before they dive in. Sometimes they aren't financially prepared to take on the full-time RVing lifestyle. You might need to save a bit before you decide to live on the road. You will need to also look into learning a budget in order to better manage your cash flow so you can sustain your new traveling lifestyle.

With enough money management, which will become easier over time, you may even decide to take your family with you on a few trips as a family vacation. It's completely possible to live on your social security income as a full-time RVer. It just takes a little time, effort, and know-how in order to do this, which will be covered later in this book.

There are a lot of resources for senior citizens who decide to pack up and take their life on the road. Most resorts, parks, campgrounds, and RV camps become like a community for those who park their RV for a period of time. As an RVer, you'll meet a variety of people from all over who are retired and decided to go out and travel for a living.

They went through some of the same processes you have with downsizing, leaving your friends and family, money management. The people of these communities can help you in your new adventure, especially if you're new to the RVing lifestyle. If you're on social media so you can see pictures of your grandchildren, you can check out RV parks and community pages.

Once you start your RVing lifestyle, you will be able to see the country and members of your family who don't live near you, such as your children and grandchildren. You'll be able to plan your trips around their schedule as much as you want to. For example, you could make sure to visit them on the holidays, their birthdays, make sure you don't miss any graduations or even school plays. You're retired now and on your RV life journey, so you get to create your own schedule and can see what you want to see.

In this book, we will discuss several topics geared towards the elderly population who are interested in starting their RVing lifestyle. The book will walk you through getting started for the RV lifestyle without any worries or hassles, choosing the right RV, managing your health on the road, budgeting your money, and ways you can earn money on the road.

Chapter 1: Choosing the Right RV to Retire Into

After you decide on the RVing lifestyle, one of your next steps is to look for the right RV to purchase. At first, you might feel overwhelmed by this because there are so many types and questions to ask yourself, such as, do you purchase a new or used RV?

This chapter will give you a start into choosing the correct RV for yourself. When you are looking to purchase an RV as a full-time traveler, you will want to handle it the same way you would handle buying a house. Take everything into consideration: will you be traveling with your children and grandchildren? What's your budget? What type of home resources will you need on the road?

Don't be shy to be as picky as you want while looking to purchase your best RV within your budget.

Different Types of RVs

Class A

Class A RVs are the most expensive and

impressive RVs on the road. But they aren't for everyone, and not always because of their 6-digit price. These RVs are for full-time travelers. So, if you are ready to sell your home, most of your belongings, and put everything you own into an RV, this type is a good choice to look at. You don't need any special license to operate them.

The pros of these RVs are they are luxurious inside and out, provide a lot of room on the inside, and tons of storage.

The cons are you will need to tow a vehicle as these RVs are tough for day trips and they are expensive to buy and repair. These RVs usually have the same options most homes do, including laundry facilities, full bath, and home entertainment systems.

Class B

Class B RVs look like a large van and are often called camper vans. These vehicles are best with only a couple of people living in them as they are a bit small inside.

These RVs contain the general basics: a shower, sink, hot water, refrigerator, air conditioning, heating.

They don't include other luxuries such as a full

bath and laundry facilities. If you are looking for an RV for just you and your significant other and don't mind missing out on some of the basic household appliances, this RV might be suitable for you.

Class C

Class C RVs reach a length of around 20 to 33 feet. If you want to travel with space similar to a Class A but cannot afford a Class A, Class C might be the way to go. It's large enough where more than a couple of people can reside comfortably and contain extra sleeping arraignments in the storage compartments or by changing the table into a bed.

Like Class A, these RVs tend to be a bit too big for day trips, so you might want to tow a vehicle but they are a little easier to drive around a campsite. Some of the longer models have a master bedroom located in the rear of the RV. They also contain a shower, regular kitchen appliances, and a great amount of storage space. If you can't afford the six figures for Class A, Class C is your best choice.

Class C might be your best option for full-time RVing, at least at first, if you are starting your new chapter but still don't have the best budget to work with. Because these RVs are cheaper to buy, repair, and easier on gas you will be able to save a bit while still living the RV lifestyle. You can always get a Class A RV later if you chose to.

Towable RVs

If you don't want to have to tow your car around with RV, you can get a towable RV. These RVs come in many different shapes and sizes with many of the same features as Class A, B, and C RVs. While towable RVs are smaller than Class A and some even Class C RVs, they still offer a lot of storage and comfort.

Usually, the largest towable RV is called the Travel Trailer and connects to the standard ball-hitch receiver. These RVs can be designed with you in mind as they can come with a full bath or just a shower and toilet. Some have areas that can expand out so you have even more room when you're stationary.

One of the biggest downfalls of this RV is they can be tough to maneuver and many people have so much trouble reversing with them attached that they don't even try. Another downfall for many people is the excessive tail swing the Travel Trailer RV can produce, especially in high winds. In fact, some people say it's safer to stay off the roads if the winds are too high.

Another type of towable RV is called the 5th Wheel Trailers. These trailers are similar to the Travel Trailer but have a gooseneck, which can make maneuvering the trailer easier, especially with high winds as the gooseneck extends over the rear of the vehicle. On top of this, the gooseneck offers more compartment storage which the travel trailer doesn't. You can get the 5th Wheel Trailer with all the modern conveniences of a house.

There are a few downsides to the 5th Wheel Trailer. First, while the trailer itself can comfortably hold you and a few of your children and grandchild, they might not all be able to fit in your vehicle. Because of the gooseneck, these trailers have to be towed by a truck with a flatbed, which limits the space available in the vehicle. No one can ride in the trailer while it's in motion because this is illegal. However, this is easy to work around if you and your significant other are the main traveling mates.

This is one of the most popular RV models for many travelers, even those who travel full-time. They like the 5th Wheel Trailer not only because they can still enjoy the modern conveniences of a home but because the price is right.

If you want a taste of the RV lifestyle but aren't sure doing it full-time is for you yet, you can looking into a foldable RV. These RVs are the smallest towable RVs and don't generally have a lot of storage space. When they aren't being used, you can fold them down so they are easier to travel with and don't take up a lot of room in the garage or in your yard. On the positive side, foldable RVs are often the cheapest and perfect size for one or two people.

Towing your Vehicle

It is cautious to invest in a towing solution that works for your RV and vehicle. A majority of RV owners overlook the need of having a towing solution. They think that an RV should not necessarily tow anything. There are three primary approaches to tow a car behind an RV.

4. Flatbed trailer (also called an enclosed trailer)

A flatbed or enclosed trailer facilitates one of the easiest ways to tow your vehicle behind larger RVs. This method offers a larger space to bring a car, off-road vehicles, or even bring in more storage to your existing RV. The flatbed or enclosed trailer provides full support for your vehicle, including its brake and light system; however, investing in a flatbed or enclosed trailer will be more expensive.

5. A tow bar

A tow bar gives you the chance to tow a vehicle behind your RV while keeping all four wheels on the road. Notably, this is one of the most common and affordable methods to tow a vehicle behind an RV. In this method, safety chains and cables are used to offer stability between the tow bar and vehicle. For safety purposes, you will need to invest in a supplemental brake system or lights. The system alerts those on the road when you turn and brake. It is critical to ensure that you can tow safely with a tow bar before investing in this solution.

6. Tow dolly

A tow dolly tows a vehicle by placing the rear wheels on the road and the front wheels on the dolly. This is meant for those who may not want to invest in an enclosed or flatbed trailer and do not want to tow using a tow bar. Nowadays, some tow dollies come with surge or electric brakes. In addition, some even come with lights, and you may not need an additional system to notify other drivers to know if you turn or brake.

It is crucial to carry out some research to determine the best fit for your towing needs. Furthermore, let your choice of towing solution align to your budget.

New Vs. Used

Year and Quality

Another question you will want to ask yourself when shopping for an RV is if you should get a new or used RV. The first rule is, no matter what type of RV if it's new or old, you will want to test everything in that RV. You can do this before you purchase it and some people often state that if you can test drive it to a location, you can test the water systems, electrical, propane systems, and other features while boondocking.

One thing to keep in mind is just because it's a used RV doesn't mean it holds less quality than a new RV. In fact, the quality of the manufacturer is more important than the year the RV was built. Because of this, some RV enthusiasts tend to look at who made the RV over what year the RV is. Buying the correct used RV can help you save thousands of dollars that you would have otherwise spent on a brand new RV.

Negotiation Tips

Many RV enthusiasts state that it's cheaper to buy an RV from a person than from the RV sales lot. But no matter who or where you buy from, there are several tips to help you get the best deal for the RV.

First, you will want to shop around. Even if you have bought from the same dealer for the last couple of decades, it never hurts to see what other deals are out there. While you shop around, compare prices and notes between the different RV dealerships as this can come in handy when you want to negotiate a price. Sometimes dealerships will bring down the price a bit just so you buy from them over their competitor.

If you want to customize your RV, you can do that later. RV enthusiasts state that it's often cheaper to buy before you customize. It's just like your home, there will always be some type of upgrades you can make. The more basic the RV is, the cheaper it will be and you can use the features your RV doesn't have during your negotiation. This is another part of your note phase. The dealership down the street might have an RV with more options for a cheaper price than the basic RV another dealer has. Using this method, you might be able to get a lower price than the dealer from down the street. You can customize your RV to your liking as you have extra money and time to do so.

A third tip is not to fall for the sign that says "sale." Often dealers mark their prices up fairly high to the Kelly Blue Book value, which means that the sale is often more money than what the RV might be worth according to Kelly Blue Book.

Do your research with the RV you're negotiating and don't be afraid to throw out a really low number. Salespeople rarely agree with the first number you throw out, so make the number about half of the asking price and then slowly increase.

A fourth tip is to buy your RV at the end of the season. Usually, campers don't sell well during certain parts of the year, such as fall. Dealerships are usually interested in making a quick sale before the weather starts to turn cold, which makes them more willing to negotiate a lower price. You want to also watch out for the quota times. Dealerships often operate on an annual or monthly basis. If they haven't sold enough RVs by the end of the cycle, they will want to sell some at a cheaper price to get rid of them.

Another tip to get a discount is to have patience. Stick to your budget and don't allow the salesperson to talk you into a higher budget or make you feel pressured to buy. Sometimes, if you take your time looking and don't buy immediately. Salespeople are more likely to work with you on negotiations because they want you to buy their product.

Financial Considerations When Buying an RV

There are several important financial factors to consider when you're in the process of purchasing your RV. Other than having a budget when buying the RV itself, the cost of insuring the RV is another factor to consider. If you buy a motorhome, you will probably have to buy special insurance and the price of the insurance will depend on the size, age, and value of the RV. If you buy a trailer, your auto insurance might cover the cost, or your insurance agency might just add a little increase to your policy.

You will also want to consider financing options when purchasing your RV. You don't need to pick the first financing company you know or see. You will want to do your research as some companies might not cover certain RVs while others might have better rates and specialty terms. You will also want to make sure that the payment plan will fit into your budget.

There are also a lot of other fees to consider when purchasing an RV, such as gas mileage, your monthly bill to maintain the RV, and any park or camping fees for when your RV is stationary.

Maintenance costs are another financial consideration when purchasing an RV. Just like a vehicle or a house, you will have to make sure there are no leaking roofs, the oil gets changed regularly, along with any filters. You'll also need to monitor the generator, water system, and electrical system. On top of this, you will have wear and tear of the furniture inside of the RV due to all the movement while driving.

Additional Factors to Consider When Obtaining an RV

Petrol or diesel

There are many advantages to purchasing an RV with a diesel engine. Diesel engines are famous for their robust nature. The engines have more power that translates to more torque, and this implies a better towing capacity and stronger uphill acceleration.

Also, diesel engines can handle a more intense, long-distance type of driving than a petrol engine. This means that a diesel engine will handle the workload better if you are using your RV full-time and moving a lot.

Nevertheless, cold weather can cause problems for diesel engines. Because of the more complex engine, you cannot take a diesel to a regular mechanic for repairs. You will require a diesel mechanic, and this may be more costly to maintain and repair.

Single vs. doubled windowpane

Some people think that replacing single-paned windows on an RV may result in a lasting insulation quality. This is not the truth since double-paned windows have a limitation that makes them impractical for use in RVs. The double-paned windows tend to fog up when subjected to strong vibrations.

Double-paned windows are not designed for use in high-vibration surroundings. If your RV does not come with standard double-paned windows, it may not be cost-effective switching them out. Moreover, if you have a travel trailer, you might want to stay away from double-paned windows altogether.

Extra points for Firsthand vs. secondhand RV

Pros of buying a firsthand RV

- You get a brand new vehicle – top of the line RV off the manufacturer's assembly line.

- Full manufacturer warranty takes effect the moment you make the purchase.

- You do not have to worry about damage or wear and tear issues when driving off for the first trip.

- You can get the exact features you want for the amount you have.

Cons of buying a firsthand RV

- It can be expensive depending on the

features present.

- One may incur more expenses in the future because the manufacturer does not customize all RVs.

- Insurance premiums for a new RV will be higher.

Pros of buying a secondhand RV

- A buyer may save a significant amount of money as compared to buying a new RV.

- One can opt to rebuild, redecorate and restore the RV to personal preference.

- Insurance premiums are lower for a secondhand RV.

- A buyer can take time to customize, repair, and upgrade existing components.

Cons of buying a secondhand RV

- Most sellers may not disclose what might be wrong with the RV.

- You may not know how depreciated the RV is in value.

- Often, the manufacturer's warranty has expired.

- One may spend a considerable amount of money on upgrades.

Note: It is cost-effective to buy a used RV when starting.

Chapter 2: How to Get Started Managing Yourself on the Road

Your Transition from Home to RV

Planning Phase

I believe its best when planning to transition from your home to your RV, you want to develop a calendar which lists your steps during the transition. You can start by setting a take-off date. While this might seem a bit far in the future, having a departure date will help set the pace and keep you on track during your planning phase.

Along with a calendar, you can also create a checklist of things you need to do before you hit the road. You will want to write down everything you can think of from finding a realtor to sell your house to researching RVs and campsites to canceling utilities.

Another way to plan is to create a vision board. Psychologically, if you can see yourself leaving for your RV life, you will believe that it will happen and it's more likely to happen. You can print out pictures of the RVs you want to look at, places you want to stay, or even paste pictures of your past travels on this board. Place this board in a location where you can see it daily as this will help you stay on track and make you more determined to reach your goals.

Join some RV traveler sites through social media. You can start to meet people who already have gone through the planning and starting out phase and ask them any questions you have and get advice.

If you haven't traveled very much in the past, you can even do some trial-runs to see if the RV life is what you really want. Sometimes you can find places that allow you to rent an RV, which might be more practical than buying one for trial trips.

Convincing Your Significant Other

One thing to remember is that this might just take time. Deciding to make the move from living in a home to becoming a full-time RVer can be scary and some people struggle with the decision more than others.

While one way to help ease any concerns your significant other might have about full-time traveling is to talk to other RVers. They might be able to help ease any fears or worries about what might go wrong and how to handle certain situations, especially emergency situations.

There are many other ways to help your significant other decide without continuing to disagree. One way is through a trial run. Take a mini trip, maybe longer than a typical week-long vacation in an RV. This might help answer any questions.

Another way is to ease into it. Maybe you decide to not sell your home and your belongings right away or maybe you put your personal items into a storage unit. Sometimes it's just the matter of not being able to let go of these things that makes someone not want the full-time RV life.

Leaving That Chapter of Your Life Behind

While some retired folks travel so they can see their children and grandchildren more, others live close to their extended family. But no matter how close or far away your family is, you can always plan to be with your family throughout your time as an RV traveler. You will just need to plan out the dates and where you need to be in order to make the family reunions, holidays, birthdays, graduations, and any other family related event you want to attend.

However, just because you can plan these dates out in your calendar, doesn't mean it'll be any less emotional. One way to help with this is to place Wi-Fi into your RV so you can use apps such as Skype or Facetime in order to see your family whenever you want. You can also use these apps to remain in close contact with your friends and remember, you will make new friends wherever you go.

Slowly detach yourself from your household items. Most of these items you have had for years and letting them go will be emotional, but you have your memories and giving the items to a thrift store or someone else will help them to create their own memories.

Budgeting For RV Living

Budgeting for RV Living is similar to creating a budget for living in a house. You want to make sure you can be able to live comfortably along with being able to manage and surprises and emergencies that can pop up. When budgeting for full-time RV living, you need to create a budget based on your income and plan. This means that any RV expenses are based on this budget. Below is a sample budget for full-time RV living. This table gives us an annual budget, including the cost of an RV. Planning in a systematic manner is the key to sticking to your budget.

Note: This table only has dummy figures, and is meant to be used as a template.

Expenses	Amount
Cost of RV	$75,000
Campground/parking	$1,900
RV Insurance	$500
Propane	$300
Cell phones	$1,000
RV registration/taxes	$100
Gas	$1,600
Diesel	$1,800

RV maintenance	$800
Vehicle maintenance	$600
Vehicle insurance	$600
Groceries/eating out	$6,000
Vehicle registration	$110
Clothing and Laundry	$800
Health Insurance	$3,000
Medical and dental expenses	$800
Miscellaneous	$2,000
Emergency/safety cushion	$7,000
Entertainment	$1,500

Total	$105,410

[1]

Of course, there are many tips to help you save money while you live your drive as a full-time RV traveler. One way is to find free camping or parking spots and do boondocking as much as possible. If you need help finding free spots across the country, there are various apps, such as Ultimate Campground and All Stays.

Another way you can help save a few dollars is to stay in one location longer. Many campgrounds and parks offer monthly and weekly rates. There are also some that might give a bigger discount if you stay a certain amount of time. You just have to ask. You should also check out various RV memberships, such as Thousand Trails, Boondockers Welcome and Passport America. These memberships can often give you discounts on various RV expenses.

Budgeting Apps

To help you monitor your budget and

---

[1] Payne, Howard, and Linda Payne. "Our 2010 Budget By Month". RV-Dreams, https://www.rv-dreams.com/2010-Budget.html..

expenses, there are a variety of apps available that you can download on your smartphone. One of the most popular ones is Mint, which is free and supports a variety of banks. If you don't like graphs or charts, your way to go is Penny. When you open the Penny app, you respond to prompts about your spending habits and summaries

Importance of an Emergency Fund

An emergency fund is some money set aside for quick and impromptu access to cover unforeseen problems. In other words, it is money that a person may earmark for expenses that come up unexpectedly. An emergency fund should be separate from retirement savings or a savings account that you may have for a specific purpose. When you start building an emergency fund, the hope is that you will never use the money; however, it will be there when you inevitably need to. Below is why you need to have an emergency fund when RVing full-time:

Surprise medical or dental expenses

Sometimes, one may get sick due to changes of weather. It is worse when you have kids and pets on board, and they develop all sorts of ailments. This kind of medical emergency requires you to have some money.

Vehicle repairs

You do not anticipate having vehicle breakdowns while on the road. Breakdowns happen at any time, especially when one least expects it. This may require you to have some money to contact the nearest gas station for repairs. Additionally, you may need some money to have a sleepover at the nearest inn if the RV breakdown is in the middle of nowhere.

It helps keep your stress levels down.

It is true that life threatens our financial wellbeing and causes stress when we face an emergency. If you do not have some money set aside for emergencies, stress will be a part of your life. Staying prepared with an emergency fund makes one confident that tackling life's unexpected events will be easy.

You do not make bad financial decisions

Having some money to attend to your emergencies helps you avoid borrowing. Even though there are various ways one can quickly access credit, the interest accrued may not be favorable. Avoiding interest on debts and maybe penalties may be best for you.

How to create one

Make cuts in your budget

Scrutinize your budget and make several cuts, especially on unnecessary expenses. While on the road, cut down any impulse purchases and ensure you buy personal effects, groceries and other foods in bulk. Within a short time, the results could raise some eyebrows.

Sell something

Do not rush to sell your home! You probably have more options than your house. Look around the house and you will be amazed to find items not in use worth the right amount. For instance, you may find old toys, exercise equipment, an old piece of furniture and many more items. You can sell such things to raise an emergency fund before you hit the road.

Make More Money

There are many opportunities to do some quick work and earn a measurable amount. Working online is one of the common ways of raising money for full-time RVers. As you work, focus on building an emergency fund.

Downsizing From Home to RV

Organizing

First, you want to organize downsizing by breaking down the process in manageable areas. This way you won't have the added stress of looking at your house as the big picture, instead, you will see it as smaller pieces. Not only will it make you feel less overwhelmed but you will be happier in the process as stress creates negative emotions, which makes you feel as if its a chore instead of a step towards your goal of becoming a full-time RVer.

One way to organize is by groups. You can sort your household items by kitchen and household items, clothing and shoes, tools and garage items, and office items. If you live out in the country, you can add another category such as outdoor items, storage items, or barn/farming items.

Items From Your House You Will Need

When you are organizing and sorting through what items you will need for your RV life and what items you won't, you'll want to remain realistic. For example, if you have a large wardrobe, figure out how often you will need dress clothes and going out clothes versus comfortable clothing. If you are planning on staying in warmer climates, such as in Florida during the winter months instead of Minnesota, you know that you won't need a lot of warm clothing. You might only keep a couple sweaters and one warmer coat.

When looking at clothing, here are some examples of clothing you will need for the full-time RV life: sandals, athletic shoes, hiking boots, sweat pants, jeans, shirt, sweater, light coat, shorts, socks, and night clothes.

Of course, there are more on the list but you can get an idea of what I usually bring. You can also downsize again after your first year of RVing. For example, if you bring a pair of dress shoes and a couple dress outfits and realize you never wore them, you can donate them. Everyone's lifestyle is different and you will realize what clothing you actually need as time goes on.

Do you still have some sentimental clothing like your wedding dress? If you can't donate it before you start traveling, you can decide to place it into storage. You might be able to donate it later or your children or grandchildren might agree to hold on to the sentimental items for you. But you want to let go of as many items as you possibly can, including the sentimental ones.

When you go into kitchen items, you will need a variety of items as you are moving from your house into the RV. You will still be cooking, washing dishes, baking, etc. But remember, you probably only need one or two spatulas instead of the ten you have in your drawer.

If you have a drawer full of silverware, you don't need all that. Just take a few items of each, enough for you and your significant other and maybe a couple more just in case you start to host company, such as your grandchildren or other RVers from the campground. Some items to think about to take with you from your kitchen include, baking pans and sheets (make sure they fit your RVs oven as some are smaller), a couple different sized pots, cups, plates, knives, spoons, forks, mugs, outdoor tablecloth, measuring cups, frying pan, and whatever else you feel you absolutely need.

From here, you continue to downsize the other areas of your home. Make sure to take only what you absolutely need.

The Utilities to have in an RV

It is prudent to keep your RV stocked with

basic supplies, non-perishable foods, linens, and clothes. This way, you will be ready to go anywhere at any time.

It is true that everyone has favorites and must-haves they cannot survive without while RVing; however, below is a list of some stock items to keep at all times while on board:

- Dishes/cooking utensils

- Pots and pans

- Heavy-duty extension cords

- Insect repellent

- Plastic bags (large and small)

- Road flares

- Rope and bungee cords

- Shovel (small folding type)

- Sports equipment

- Adapters for 30 amp and 50 amp outlets

- Batteries

- Binoculars

- Bottle/can opener

- Camera and memory cards

- Soap and toiletries

- Sunscreen

- Jacket/raincoat

- Maps and GPS

- RV toilet paper

- Matches/lighter

- Nature field guides

- Pillows, blankets, sheets

- Picnic basket

- Firewood

- First-aid supplies

- Flashlights, lanterns

- Folding chairs

- Grill and fuel

- Toolkit

- Towels

- Trash bags

- Umbrellas

- Water hose (white potable water type)

Before you hit the road, ensure you balance your load and avoid over-packing. Keep in mind the weight label on your RV.

Decluttering

Once you have completed the process of finding household items you need, you can go through all the items again and see if you can downsize more. Throughout your downsizing process, you will want to continue to donate items, sell them, or put them in the trash. If you kept years of papers and receipts you no longer need, shred and recycle them.

There will be a lot of items you put in the keep pile that you placed there for sentimental value. This is completely normal but it's not a reason to absolutely keep the item.

There are some items you can probably continue to hold, like maybe your great-grandma's wedding ring if you aren't ready to pass that onto your daughter or granddaughter, but most of the items should be donated, given to family, or sold.

Remember, you are starting a brand new chapter in your life and it's a great time to start decluttering your home so you can start this brand new chapter fresh.

Every family has treasured photographs and some go back a hundred years or so. Of course, these photographs won't mean anything to anyone else but yourself and they aren't meant to be sold. You don't need to throw them away to make room either.

While your RV has room for a few pictures or one photo album, the best process is to scan the items onto your computer through a USB drive, an online service, or an external hard drive. For the old photographs, once they are scanned, you can bring them to your local historical society. The staff at museums love to take a family's treasured photographs and preserve them for future generations. But first, you should see if any other members of your family would want the photographs.

If you have items you don't want to let go of because of sentimental value, you could always take a picture of it and save it onto your computer with your other photographs. While you won't have the physical object anymore, you will have a photograph of your treasured item that you can view at any moment.

Another tip to decluttering those sentimental items is to give them away to your friends and family you won't see as often. Not only is this a way that you know these items will be well taken care of, and you will be able to see them again when you visit, but it's also a way your loved ones can hold onto memories with you.

Selling, Donating and Disposing of Clutter

There are a variety of ways outlets to help you get rid of your clutter. While there are some things you will end up recycling or throwing, most of it you will be able to sell, donate and give to family and friends. One of the biggest tricks is to know what to do with what item.

There are different ways to sell items. Of course, one of these ways is to have a garage sale or take part in a community-wide rummage sales. Most communities have these, usually happening during the summer months of May- September.

Some communities have more than one throughout the year. Take advantage of these as much as you can. People tend to come from all over the area because there are so many people selling their items at once. If you live in a town, you have the best advantage to hosting your own garage sale. You can do this once a month or even once a week. People love garage sales and often look for the signs at the corner of the street, providing your city allows this, or flyers hanging up.

Social media gives you another great advantage of selling your items. Not only can you advertise your garage sales on social media, such as Facebook, but you can also join area swap and shops.

Several areas have groups like these where people post their items for sale and whoever wants to buy them comments and then people usually find a way to meet because they live in the same area. One thing to remember is to be cautious about this and don't invite too many people over to your house.

It's often safer to meet in a public location, such as a grocery store parking lot in the middle of the day. To use Facebook sell groups, you will need to have an account. This is free for anyone with an email or a cell phone. All you need to do to see if your areas have a for sale site is to search your location into Facebook's search bar and the page should show up.

Another way to get rid of items is to donate them. Local thrift stores are a great outlet for this. People from all over tend to shop at thrift stores not only because they are cheaper than regular stores but because the items in thrift stores are unique and personalize their homes. For clothing, shoes, and some other household items, you can always donate to homeless or other types of shelters. They are usually in need of various clothing sizes and shoes.

There are also items that you will probably just end up recycling or throwing. If you have limited garbage space and it's only picked up once a week, you could contact your city to see if you can rent a dumpster for a period of time. Also, one of the best time to focus on decluttering is during a city clean-up week. Most cities have these and if yours does, it's a great way to get rid of all your old belonging you are going to throw. You just put these items on your curb and on a certain day, the garbage man will pick them up without any extra charge for the extra garbage.

Choosing Your Domicile

Your domicile is the place you plan to return, your legal residence. As a full-time traveler, you pick your domicile and follow their laws and guidelines when getting your mail, vote, pay taxes, etc. Deciding on your state will have many effects for your full-time traveling life from how much taxes you pay to insurance rates.

While you can pick any state, Texas, Florida, and South Dakota are the three states which are more domicile friendly. There are also many states which require you to live there a certain amount of time in order to establish domicile.

You will want to look into death with dignity laws when choosing your domicile. Death with Dignity laws allow you to end your life through voluntary self-administration if you become terminally ill while traveling.

The Best State to Register your RV

When you fail to do your research concerning the best state to register your RV in, the whole process may be a difficult situation. The first requirement is declaring a state as your primary residence. It would be best if you tried to find a state that has its taxation system set up to your advantage.

Without a doubt, you have eliminated all except the following nine states:

- Tennessee

- Texas

- Washington

- Wyoming

- Alaska

- Florida

- Nevada

- New Hampshire

- South Dakota

Even though Tennessee and New Hampshire do not have an income state, they tax interest income and dividends; therefore, we can leave them off the friendly list.

Generally, you have to pass through the state occasionally to renew your vehicle registration, and driver's license. This makes Alaska off the list of the states above. The state is tax-friendly, but making an annual pilgrimage that far north may be extreme for some people.

Having struck off Alaska, Tennessee and New Hampshire from the list, we are down to six friendly possibilities. Concerning sales tax, there is not much difference between the remaining six states.

The personal property tax will affect the process of RV possessions. Which states have personal property tax? Among the remaining six states, Florida and Washington have a personal property tax; thus, we drop two more out of the list of full-time RV-friendly states.

Therefore, the final four possibilities are:

- Nevada

- South Dakota

- Texas

- Wyoming

How to Receive Mail while Living in an RV

How do you survive when you are on the road without a physical fixed home address? It is never that complicated receiving your mail while still RVing.

You will never realize how important a mail delivery is, until when you are living away from home. Mail sent to your home address is delivered to your doorstep, and the only task is to pick them up. What happens to your letters when you choose an RV lifestyle?

Below, we discuss ways you can receive your mail while living in an RV:

Use of mail forwarding services

An RVer lifestyle comes with a lot of freedom because no-one wants to keep waiting for his or her mail for a long time. There are popular companies that offer mail-forwarding services. In most cases, the help you get a home address. Even so, the companies also offer the services to people who live as fulltime RVers. They deliver mails to the park where one may be camping. This is possible because most RV parks ask for your address. This way, mails delivered to the park can be sorted out to respective mail addresses.

Pick a provider that you trust to give you services that fit your RV. Comprehend the pros and cons of each method you are about to choose. You can always call your service provider to inform you what is in your mail at a small cost.

Receiving mail through family or friends

Many RVers use family and loved ones to receive their mail. All you need to do is to ensure whoever is forwarding the mail to you is organized and efficiently delivers the mail to you on time.

When RVing and on a tight budget, using family to receive mail will be a great way of saving on costs. The disadvantage with this method is in case many letters come every day, as it might be a bit difficult to forward them.

Your mail might also be mishandled and delayed. It is advisable to have your email repackaged into one parcel and forwarded. While in an RV, you will need to maintain clear communication with your family so they know the exact location to send your mail to.

Using mailboxes at UPS stores

UPS stores offer a full package of business and communication services including shipping, packing and delivery services. UPS is something to consider when selecting a solution for your RV lifestyle since they offer personal packages and handle mail carefully.

With UPS, you generally find a post office near a place you would like your mail delivered to. The challenge with this method is that it is expensive and not recognized as a legal address.

Campground deliveries

Many inventions have come up, for example, Amazon Prime for RVers. They usually have mail delivered to RV parks with two days shipping guaranteed. If your other options for mail deliveries cannot work for you, consider trying out this one.

All you need is to let the service providers know where your campground is and they will call you once your mail is delivered.

Getting mail on the road may not be as difficult as many think.

When You Start on the Road Full-Time

RV Parks and Senior Campgrounds

One of the best ways to find parks and campgrounds that are for seniors is to do a little research.

There are a variety of websites which will give you various senior parks to stay during the RV chapter of your life. One of these is Alligator Park RV Park in Florida. This park allows both part-time and full-time RVers and is one of the RV friendly states.

This community holds many events from

playing games to community potlucks. You will have tons of opportunities to meet and get to know the people around you who have also started the RV chapter of their lives. Many people who have stayed here note that the price is fair and it's clean.

The Bentsen Grove Resort in Texas is great for those who want to stay in the south during the cold winter months of the north. This place not only offers all the comforts of a retirement community but is also close to the Mexican border and many cities which allow you to purchase the necessities you need without having to travel too far.

Mission View RV Resort is located in Tucson, Arizona, with a variety of picnic tables and patios for your outdoor desires. This senior RV community also has its own clubs, pools, library, and ballroom for events.

Colorado is another state that has several RV parks dedicated to senior citizens. In these parks, you will find all the hookups you need for your RV, planned events such as barbeques, family areas, hot tubs, and pools. That state has carefully planned these parks all around Colorado so you can pick which park you stay at by your interests. For example, if you're looking for a more calm and beach-type park, they have that. If you want one that's closer to a major city, that's available.

There are dozens more RV parks and campgrounds that are not only senior citizen-centered but have built the area like a retirement community so you have a one-stop shop for the things you need with entertainment provided. In some of these communities, you only need to leave your RV location if you want to venture to other areas for sightseeing or to find different stores for your necessities.

Boondocking

Boondocking is just another term for dry RVing or parking in a designated and independent location and using the amenities as they are available.

While some people feel boondocking isn't safe, others feel it's safer being out in the wilderness than being in a city where crime is more likely to occur. But if you're still worried about your first boondocking trip, there are several things you can do to help your mind feel more at ease.

First, remember, your home is one wheel and if you feel uncomfortable in a location, you can leave. When boondocking, you're free to come and go as you wish. Also, make sure to keep your keys and phone next to you, just in case there is an emergency. You can also keep a heavy-duty flashlight and loud fog horn.

If you're wondering where you can legally boondock, you will just need to look for the designated areas that allow boondocking. Many of the locations are managed by the National Forests or other governmental groups that have set up these free camping sites on public lands. They are designated for this purpose and people will encourage you to stay in these areas if you want to boondock. To find these areas, you can easily use Google or find apps, such as Public Lands app or Ultimate Campgrounds.

If you're in your planning phase and still looking at what RV to purchase for your RV lifestyle and know you want to boondock as much as possible for long periods of time in order to help save money, you will want to consider the size of your holding tank on your RV. You will also want to make sure to consider supplies, once you get to this point. Of course, you will have another way to get around, whether it's your RV or your vehicle, but it never hurts to make sure you're well prepared when boondocking.

If you're going to boondock and work at the same time--we will discuss working as an RV traveler later in this book--you will want to think about electricity.

One of the ways to gain electricity while boondocking is through the use of solar power, which is something you can consider when purchasing your RV. If you don't want to get into the big solar power world yet, you can start with a portable solar panel, which isn't generally too expensive. Of course, another way to go is through the use of a generator.

Weather is one thing you will want to consider when you are boondocking. For your own safety, you'll probably not want to think about boondocking when it's below 40 degrees or above 90 degrees. Of course, the temperature is up to your preferences. Some people handle the heat or cold better than others.

Another major piece to consider when boondocking is water. Boondockers usually do a variety of things to conserve water. Some RV boondockers have installed a shutoff valve and shut their water off when they aren't using it. They also install a low flowing shower head, which helps conserve water. You can also purchase a low flowing water faucet for your sink to help you save on more water. On top of this, you can also purchase solar showers, which are a lot easier to bring into town if you need to refill it.

In order to avoid a lot of trash, you can easily stock your fridge up with fresh foods that don't give you a lot of messy trash. For the trash you have, you can keep them in a closed bin that isn't hanging around outside for animal to smell and find. Then, when you make trips into town, you simply bring your trash with you and dump it in a city dumpster. You can do the same thing with anything you want to recycle as several cities house a recycling center of some type.

Join Groups and Meet New People

Get out and meet as many people in the parks and campgrounds as you can. Not only will they become a sense of support for your new lifestyle, but they can offer you tips and advice on how to live your RV life to the best of your abilities. You will find that the people you meet come from a variety of cultures and backgrounds, which can make RVing more enjoyable.

When staying at the RV parks and

campgrounds, remember to check out any groups that the community has for full-time RVers. You can also go onto your social media accounts and meet people who also live the full-time RV life.

Chapter 3: Healthcare and Insurance

Healthcare and insurance are important for everyone, but especially senior citizens. Unfortunately, as we age, our health begins to deteriorate, even if we feel just as young as we did 20 years ago. On top of this, you never know what type of health issues are going to pop up and when. Health insurance can help cover the cost of any medication you need. Health insurance can also help cover costs for regular physicals and any other type of annual health tests and reviews. The older we get, the more testing doctors say we need to have completed so we can continue to live our happiest and greatest lives for as long as possible.

You are about to live or just started living a new and fun chapter in your life as an RV traveler, don't neglect your health to put it to a stop.

Healthcare Options and Plans for RVing Seniors and Retirees

Medicare and Medigap Plans

When you are traveling around the country, you aren't sure where you're going to be when a health emergency might happen or when you need to get to your next physical. While it's easier to plan around physicals and annual testing, it's still important to make sure you have coverage that is nationwide. This is why I advise that RVing seniors and retirees get a plan under Medicare or Medigap.

Medicare and Medigap plans work together. Medicare is your major health insurance while Medigap covers the gaps that Medicare doesn't cover. For instance, on average, Medicare covers about 80% of the costs approved by Medicare. If you have Medigap, this plan will normally come in and cover around 20% that Medicare doesn't cover. These two plans are designed to work together and if you are eligible, it's best to get the plans together.

First, to become eligible to the Medicare and Medigap plan, you need to be over the age of 65. You also need to be a legal resident of the United States or at least have a Green card for no less than five years. You can also become eligible for this plan if you have a disability.

Every year, there is a six month enrollment period, which is the best time to enroll. However, if you miss the enrollment period, you can still sign up under certain conditions. These two conditions are if you left your job and are now left without health insurance, or you can sign up during the general enrollment period.

And don't worry about if you have a pre-existing condition because Medigap will still approve you if you have a pre-existing condition. Usually, people believe that you can only get this plan if you have already applied for Social Security benefits. This isn't true. You're still eligible for this plan if you haven't applied for your Social Security benefits.

Sometimes people are automatically enrolled in Medicare, but then you want to make sure you're enrolled in Medigap too. You can sign up for either through a few websites, such as AARP and SocialSecurity.gov.

You can also call the Social Security office or contact AARP if you have any questions. Both of these services are a great way to find out more about your health insurance options, plans, and enrollment.

Medicare Plans, Requirements, and Companies. Which is Best for You?

Medicare Medical Savings Account (MSA) Plan

The Medicare Medical Savings Account plan is a certain type of savings account where money is deposited into your medical savings account and you can use this money when you need to for healthcare reasons prior to meeting your deductible. This plan covers all the Medicare Advantage Services plans and can also cover vision, dental, and long-term care, which aren't always covered by Medicare.

There are about ten steps when you use this type of Medicare plan. The first step is you want to pick a high deductible plan because these plans only work with high deductibles. Next, you will set up your account with a ban, which is usually chosen by the insurance company. You will receive the amount of money designated to you by Medicare. You can this use this money as you need to for medical related expenses. The key to remember is that once this money is gone, you won't be able to receive more until the next year. However, if you don't use up all the funds, they will remain in your account. It's not a use it or lose it savings plan.

The money in your account can be used for expenses covered by your plan or expenses that aren't covered by your plan. You won't be turned away from using this card for any medical related expenses. Whenever you use this money, it's counted towards your plan's deductible. If you run out of money in your savings account before you reach your deductible, then any other medical related expenses you will need to pay out of your own pocket.

Finally, one important piece to remember is anything you spend this money on needs to be recorded for tax purposes. When you do your taxes, you will want to fill out Form 8853, which allows the IRS to see where the money from your medical savings account went to.

Plan F

The most comprehensive Medicare plans are Plan F and are available in most states. However, because Plan F covers a wide variety of services, its premiums are generally on the higher range. On the plus side, with this plan, your beneficiaries will have little to no remaining bills for any medical related events or hospital stays.

The range of benefits and costs associated with Plan F are skilled nursing facility coinsurance, Medicare Part B coinsurance, excessive charges, and deductible. Plan A deductible, and hospice care copayment or coinsurance are also a part of this plan.

Plan G

Supplemental insurance, Plan G helps to cover all out-of-pocket expenses from other Medicare Plans A and B. For example, Plan G would cover for coinsurance, copayments, and other charges. Many people don't even have to pay a monthly premium because they paid into this plan while they were working. Plan G is known to cover more of the out-of-pocket Medicare expenses than other supplemental insurance plans. Like Plan F, Plan G covers 100 % of Plan B Medicare expenses, however, it doesn't cover all of Plan A. Plan F and Plan G cover the same excess charges under Plan A. The costs for this plan depends on where your domicile is located and not all states have to offer this plan.

High Deductible Plan F

The High Deductible Plan F is a version of Plan F. In this plan, you will pay all the fees until you reach your deductible. You might also be able to enroll in this plan for a cheaper monthly payment than the standard Plan F. However, the prices for the monthly payment can depend on where you domicile is located. This plan also makes your beneficiaries pay high out-of-pocket expenses. But once your deductible is reached, then the healthcare company will pay for the rest of your expenses.

Medical Savings Account Plan

The Medical Savings Account Plan is similar to the Medicare Medical Savings Account plan but this plan is often paid into while you are working. You can then receive the money for medical related expenses when you need them. This plan generally works with a high deductible. These plans don't allow Medicare drug coverage, so you will probably want to find a supplemental plan to help cover your prescriptions.

Medicare Advantage Plan

This plan provides all your Medicare Part A and Part B plans. There are six different types of Medicare Advantage plans available. The first is the Private Fee for Service Plans. These plans allow you to go to any doctor or hospital. They determine how much they will pay the hospital, doctors, and other healthcare providers and how much you will need to pay out of your own pocket once you get the care.

Thes second Medicare Advantage Plan is the Health Maintenance Organization, also known as an HMO, plan. These plans state you can only go to health care providers that are included in your service. In addition, you will need to get a referral from your primary care doctor if you need to see specialists outside of the plan's service providers.

Special Needs plans is another type of Medicare Advantage Plan which gives assistance to a special group of people, such as people who live in a nursing home, retirement community, have both Medicare and Medicaid, or diagnosed with certain medical conditions.

Preferred Provider Organization, also known as a PPO is a type of plan which allows you to pay less if you use medical providers which are covered under the plan. If you go to a medical provider who isn't covered under the plan, you will pay more.

Finally, there is an HMO Point of Service plan which will help you get some medical services that are not covered but you will need to pay a higher copayment or coinsurance.

In order to join Medicare Advantage Plan, your domicile needs to be located within the plan's selected service area and some pre-existing conditions will not make you eligible for these plans. These health insurance plans run on a monthly premium, which varies from plan to plan.

Medigap Plans

In total, there are ten Medigap Plans with each one a little different from the next. Each one is a supplemental insurance plan designed to cover areas that your main health insurance doesn't. While state and federal laws might make an insurance company sell specific Medigap plans, typically, each company can pick which plans they can sell. However, the only states that are different from what plans they sell are Massachusetts, Minnesota, and Wisconsin. All other states are consistent with the plan standards and what the sell.

All ten plans have the same basic benefits, some differ slightly as to how much they cover. For instance, all the ten plans, Plan A through Plan N cover Part A hospital and coinsurance costs up to a year after the patient has met his or her deductible. But, eight out of the ten plans cover all of Part B copayment or coinsurance. The two that don't cover all of that benefit is Plan K, which only covers 50% and Plan L, which will only cover 75%. This is the same for the following benefits, first three pints of blood, Part A hospice care coinsurance or copayment, and coinsurance for skilled nursing facility care.

Under Medigap plans, the benefit of Part A deductible is not covered by Plan A and only half covered by plans K and M. Plan L covers 75% of Part A deductible. The benefit of Part B deductible is only covered by Plans C and F. Medigap Plans F and G are the only ones to cover the benefit of Plan B excess charge. Medigap Plans A, B, K, and L don't cover the benefit of Foreign travel exchange but the rest of the plans will cover 80%.

The most popular Medigap plan is F, which costs around $326 per month. It's highly recommended that before you sign papers to buy any of these plans, you contact your state's insurance department as they will help you select the right plan for you. Because they are similar, it can be a bit difficult and confusing in which plan will best fit you and your main health insurance. You will also want to make sure that the company selling the plans are licensed to be able to sell these plans and the state's insurance department can give you this information.

Finding Healthcare on the Road

If you need to see a doctor for whatever reason, find the closest hospital or clinic and call them. Even if your insurance won't be covered by them, they might have payment options and discounts. Clinics and hospitals will always work with people and it's much more important to be seen than to ignore your symptoms and continue on your journey.

If you have nationwide coverage but you're still not sure if the closest clinic or hospital will work with your insurance, you can still call them. They might also be able to give you information on a nearby location where your insurance will be covered.

If you don't know where the closest hospital or clinic is, you can call various areas in the location you're at and they will help you. Social Service centers are a great resource along with any tourist location or city halls. Many Social Service centers have their own clinics, which are usually designed for people without health insurance or people whose health insurance won't cover them at the local hospital or clinic. These special clinics are designed to work with you and are generally much cheaper than regular clinics or hospitals. And, contrary to popular belief, they have the same services and can handle your situation as well as any other hospital or clinic.

Obtaining Medicare through the United States Veterans Administration

If you are a veteran of the United States, you should look into obtaining health insurance through their program first. The Veterans Administration often has better rates and benefits designed for veterans. The majority of veterans will cover for the free- healthcare but some will need to pay a coinsurance or copayment for medical services. If you get the Veterans Administration's healthcare insurance, you don't need to worry about supplemental insurance because VA insurance covers all the benefits.

There are many requirements for being approved for VA health insurance. For instance, you need to have served for two straight years if you enrolled for active duty before September 7, 1980, and after October 16, 1981. You can't have received a dishonorable discharged and you need to prove with the DD-214 papers of your discharge.

Obtaining Medication on the Road

One of the biggest tricks full-time RVers use with medication is to get a 90 day supply of their medications. You can also get medication sent to your through your mail, which is how the majority of RVers receive their medications. Most pharmacies will approve of this and it makes it easier as you are traveling.

Another tip is to use a chain pharmacy store, such as CVS, Walgreens, or Walmart to get your medications filled. Your information will be in their systems and any pharmacists who work for these companies can look up your information and get your prescriptions refilled. Pharmacists can also contact your doctor if you need to get refills on your prescriptions.

There are ways to get an emergency refill if you are ever in a jam. While this can easily be avoided but just paying attention and staying ahead, things happen and you might end up needing a refill quickly. If this happens, the best thing to do is to take your prescription bottle or any documentation to a local pharmacy. Sometimes, they are able to help you. If the pharmacy doesn't cover your health insurance, you will need to pay for the prescriptions out of your pocket. However, you can always call your healthcare insurance company or go online to their website to file an insurance claim.

Keep Your Insurance Updated

One of the most important things to remember is to keep your medical history updated when you're on the road. You never know what will happen when and a doctor who doesn't know your history or what medications you're on can't treat you properly. You will want to update your records every time you get a test done or anything else changes or gets added to your report. You can do this very simply with the technology of today's world, such as through your laptop. You'll want to remember to keep it on a USB or external hard drive so the doctor can view it on the hospital if need be.

It wouldn't be a bad idea to have a backup somewhere of your medical information, just in case something doesn't work with the technology you use. While you want to keep what you have in your RV to a minimum, your medical history is pretty important, so it wouldn't hurt to have a physical copy safely put away in your RV, and make sure your significant other knows where the papers are. If you are traveling alone then you can always keep a little note of where the papers are close to your driver's license or another form of ID authorities will use to identify you if an emergency ever occurs. It's always better to be safe than sorry, especially when it comes to your health.

Finding the Best Insurance

Not only is finding the right healthcare insurance important for anyone but it's even more important for a senior citizen. Finding health insurance can also be a bit more challenging for you when you have decided to become a full-time RVer. Many believe that it's often the health insurance cost that will really determine if you can financially afford to become a full-time RVer or not.

One of the best ways to find health insurance that is right for you is to check out the plans through the Affordable Care Act. This act is the best not only because you want nationwide coverage but also because you might be self-employed while on the road to make a little extra income.

When searching for the best plan, you will want to pay attention to the wide area it covers as you will want it to cover where you travel as much as possible. You'll also want to find out what plans are in your state of domicile as you will need to get health insurance which is dependent on your state. If you haven't decided on your state of domicile yet, maybe decide through looking into the healthcare plans for full-time RVers.

One of the best states to provide the cheapest and best healthcare of full-time RVers is Florida. They have a variety of plans, such as Florida Blue, which offers great benefits for travelers.

One of the most useful sites for full-time RVers is rverinsurance.com. The person behind the site is a man named Kyle Henson. Not only is Henson a full-time RVer himself, but he is also an insurance agent. This website will not only keep you up to date on all the ongoings in the Medicare world but he will also help you find the right plan.

Sources of Medical Information

The following are a list of the best sources found for medical information pertaining to senior citizens

https://www.aarp.org/health/medicare-insurance/

AARP is one of the best sources for medical insurance for the elderly. Not only do they provide information on all the plans available, but they also have a list of common questions and answers. Of course, they're always available to answer your questions or give advice.

https://www.medicare.gov/

Medicare.gov is the main source for all your Medicare needs. This website is the United States Government's official Medicare site.

https://www.ssa.gov/benefits/medicare/

The official website for the Social Security Administration also offers very useful and up to date information on all Medicare health insurance information.

Chapter 4: Making Money on the Road

Many full-time RVers, even the ones who retired before they started to travel, make a little money doing various jobs while on the road. These jobs are usually not very time consuming and often start out due to hobbies the individual had. For example, many RVers tend to run their own website blogs where they discuss their travels and give advice for new RV travelers.

There are dozens of jobs available to those who travel full-time. Of course, some local places will have job service agencies that you can go to, however, most of these jobs tend to deal with manual labor and this isn't an option for everyone. Below is a list of ideas for full-time RVers who are interested in making a little income through Freelance or other means while on the road.

The jobs that are available to full-time RVing senior citizens often depends on what type of skills or education you have. While most jobs will be able to train you without much experience, there are some jobs where campgrounds might want some experience and others where they might want some sort of education.

Jobs for Seniors and Retirees

Amazon Camperforce Work Opportunities

Amazon is one of those companies that are quick to catch on to the latest trends going on in the world. When they realized that a good amount of the American population, including the elderly, were traveling full-time in an RV they decided to take advantage of this. Amazon is already a huge company and they seem to be growing more and more every day, which means they are always looking for help.

Not too long ago, Amazon created a new program called Amazon CamperForce. The company designed this program specifically for RVers who are in search of a job. One of the perks about this job is it's located in various parts of the country, so if they hired you at one campsite they could hire you at another. On top of this, they understand that you're not going to stay in one spot for very long. Another perk is you have a say in if you want to just work seasonally or if you want to work in a variety of Amazon CamperForce locations.

All Amazon CamperForce employees make at least $15 per hour. The company also has a variety of benefits for their employees, such as 401(K), overtime pay, Prescription and medical coverage after working for the company for 90 days, assignment completion bonus, up to $550 a month per campsite, and a weekly pay schedule. They are located in states such as Kentucky, Tennessee, and Arizona. You can go to their website, amazondelivers.jobs/about/camperforce/ and find out what positions are open and where.

Campground Host

Another job you can do as a full-time RVer is a campground host. These jobs are typically seasonal but if you travel from campground to campground throughout the year, you might be able to stay employed most of the time. When you're hired to be a campground host, you can sometimes decide where you want to work as a campground usually hires a bunch of different hosts. For example, some might work in stores, manage canoe rentals, boat rental, or hiking trails. There might be other types of jobs available, depending on the type of campground you are at.

There are also various other smaller jobs if you don't want one with a lot of responsibility because you have recently retired and want to do more relaxing than working. Some of these types of jobs would include, answering questions for guests, helping guests solve problems, welcoming new residents and guests, collecting fees, preparing weekly revenue, preparing attendance reports, and cleaning exterior and interior buildings.

A benefit of being a campground host is you will reside in your own RV and not have to leave the campground to go to work. If you are interested in becoming a campground host you can either talk to your campground manager as they might have duties you can do or you can go on the internet to www.camphost.org. Not only does this website discuss what a camp host does, but it also allows to see various campgrounds that have these types of jobs available. There are only a few states which are on the website. These states include Minnesota, Arizona, Alabama, California, Florida, Tennessee, New York, Michigan, and Wisconsin.

You can also apply for a job through the website, join their social media group on facebook, and also join their mailing list.

Seasonal Work

Of course, we have already discussed some seasonal work, but there is a lot more. Sometimes, you just need to look around in the area you are in as there might be seasonal work that you unaware of until you ask around.]

Other season work includes holiday stores. There are some stores, especially in bigger cities, which are only open during certain holidays. Some of these stores include Halloween and Christmas stores. These stores are used to hiring people on a temporary basis, so you don't have to worry about explaining to your boss that you travel for a living and might not be around for a very long time. You could also find a job at a Christmas Tree farm or on a farmer's market. There might also be major flea markets in the area which are looking for people to handle concession stands or other booths.

Property caretakers are another form of seasonal work, but work that you can also find year round if you want to. For instance, you might travel to the northern states during the summer months and then travel more south during the winter months. Both of these areas will have people looking for property caretakers.

While the jobs for property caretakers tend to vary from one person to the next as it's generally whatever they want to be completed, the jobs usually focus on yard work. For example, you could be mowing the lawn, raking leaves, weeding, and taking care of their garden. They also might ask you to take care of the housekeeping, such as coming in to clean once or twice a week. The homeowners might also ask you to do various odd jobs for them, such as getting their mail or going grocery shopping.

Tax preparation is also another seasonal job which RVers can do. In this day and age, you wouldn't even have to leave your RV in order to work for a tax firm. Some places might ask for on-site training, but many will train remotely if they hire someone to work remotely.

Amusement parks are another season job which is a good choice for RVers. These areas usually have different types of jobs available from running game stands to running rides to managing concession stands. Some places also look for people to play a part in the entertainment section, whether they play someone on a ride or some other entertainment.

Park Manager

Because you often stay at parks or campgrounds while traveling as a full-time RVer, one of the best ways to see if there is any work for you is to ask the people who own or manage the place you are staying at.

Just like a campground host, you could find a job working as a park manager. These jobs are sometimes similar to a campground host but can also contain more responsibilities, such as paperwork and budgeting.

Other duties you might have to take care of as a park manager are collecting the rent from other travelers, perform meter readings, know some minor computer skills, and oversee other people working at the park.

Not only will these type of jobs often give you an hourly wage or salary, but they will also include some benefits for you as you reside and work at the park.

Activities Director

Previously, we discussed how many of the RV senior campgrounds and parks run like a retirement community. They often have a busy entertainment schedule full of games, such as bingo, cards, and other types of entertainment.

There is always a person behind the curtain who is coming up with ideas for the activities around the site and getting them ready for the residents who will be participating. This person's title is Activities Director and chances are if your campground or park hosts a variety of activities, they have one of these positions.

Sometimes these positions not only have you schedule and host the events, but they will also give you other responsibilities, such as maintaining and managing recreational needs. In order to know exactly what activities the campground or park is capable of, you will need to know the inventory of what the park has. You will also be in charge of letting someone know if you need any supplies for an event or ordering the supplies yourself.

You will also be in charge of making sure all of the guests at the park or campground are aware of the activities, when they are, and where they are. One of the best ways people have done this creates a monthly calendar.

This way, residents know what is going on and can sometimes plan their errand run or other things around the events. If you create a calendar, it's important to remember to get this calendar to new guests who have arrived after the calendar has gone out so they can find the events and meet new people. Sometimes people want to hire activities directors who have some sort of experience with organization and event planning. They will also want to hire someone who has customer service skills and handles communicating with people well.

Park Groundskeeper

A Park Groundskeeper is someone who works at the park or campsite and takes care of the maintenance around the location. Of course, if it's a big site, there will probably be more than one groundskeeper and you will be assigned a certain section. However, some places are small enough where you will manage all the tasks. These can include such jobs as mowing the lawn, cleaning the pool, raking leaves, tending to a garden, picking up trash, and making sure all the guests are following the rules and guidelines. You could also assist in the maintenance of buildings and help prepare the RV lot after a guest leaves.

Some of these jobs offer benefits, such as paid holidays, PTO, 401(k), and even healthcare. The average hourly rate for these type of job ranges from $10 to $16 per hour. This type of job could usually be a trainable job without much prior experience, except maybe what you completed at your own home before you began traveling.

Campground Cook

The one thing about a place where there are people is chances are pretty good there will be a kitchen which needs staff to cook, clean, and make sure people get the meals they came for.

Campgrounds and parks usually have a certain number of cooks to help make sure mealtimes run smoothly. Sometimes they split the jobs into dessert or main meals. Sometimes you are hired to help for one meal throughout the day. For example, you might be hired to help with breakfast but not have to worry about helping with lunch or supper.

Of course, whenever you work in a kitchen, there are a variety of rules and guidelines you need to follow. Some of these are part of government health code regulations, such as wearing a hairnet and gloves when you are in the kitchen. If you enjoy cooking or baking, you might want to contact the campground or park before you head there to see if there will be a job available for you once you reach your destination.

To be a campground cook, you might have to

go through a certain training session or two where you cook for someone. They might want to know your experiences in cooking, such as if you've ever had a job similar or what your interest is with cooking and baking.

Outdoor Tour Guide

One of the things most RV parks and campgrounds focus on is making sure new guests feel as comfortable as possible and know where things are. Sometimes, parks and campgrounds hold some type of orientation where new guests are taken around the grounds so they know where they kitchen, activities area, store, and other areas on the grounds are. The people who give these tours are often known as outdoor tour guides.

Unless you are an outdoor tour guide in a really busy park or campground, this job might be on an as-needed basis. Sometimes, this job might actually be tied to another position, such as groundskeeper.

Outdoor tour guides are usually trained with their job and often given several guidelines to follow. For example, if your campground has hiking trails, you might need to not only show where these trails are but explain the dos and don'ts of the trails.

Other Work Opportunities

There are various other work opportunities that you can find while on the road. These jobs will vary from one campsite to the other. For instance, you might find that one campground is looking for a photographer because they are working on developing a new brochure. They might want to hire guests of the site, even if they aren't professional photographers because they have stayed on the grounds and can give a personal tale of the campground. For this job, you might not need to have hardly any skills in photography, you just might need your own camera and to take a certain number of pictures in a variety of areas.

Another work opportunity for full-time RVers is called telecommuting. This is a job service which became popular because of the number of RVers that work from their homes. These opportunities offer a variety of positions, such as telemarketing, web developer, computer programmer, graphic artist, data entry clerk, recruiter, bookkeeper, and medical transcriptionist. While some of these jobs will require people to have a strong understanding of the job, others might be more of a training session or two before you start working by yourself.

If you are a creative person, you can always create something to sell online. For example, if you make jewelry, you can go on websites such as Etsy and sell your jewelry. This doesn't require any other special skills than what you already have and know. On top of this, all you need to do is get Paypal so you can be paid and a person's address so you know where to send it to. You can send mail through any Post Office, FedEx, or UPS location.

Freelancing

There are many types of freelancing jobs on the internet. One of the most popular places to find a freelancing job is through Upwork. This site offers a variety of jobs for decent pay. This site is good for nearly any freelancer, whether you are a writer, artist, book designer, editor, transcriptionist, or another job. You never know what types of jobs Upwork has until you sign up, get approved, and start searching.

The one downside to Upwork is the site has become so popular that their guidelines for getting accepted have narrowed. For example, if you are one of 200 people who recently signed up with the skillset of writing and editing, you might not be approved because Upwork could see they have too many people with the same skillset. If this happens, you can always try to get approved later. You could also write down all your skills and create a different mix where Upwork might approve you because your skillset is more varied and not a lot of people have the same skillset as you.

What type of experience you have depends on the job. There are some employers on Upwork who want their employees to have some experience while there are others that will take people at a beginner's level of experience. You will generally know what the employer is looking for because of the description of what they of experience they want will be included.

Another freelancing site is called GoTranscript. This site is a transcription service that pays you about $0.72 per minute. This site will train all their staff, so you don't need to have any previous experience.

YouTube

While it can take a while to make money off of YouTube, it is possible and there are tons of RVers who make their income by posting YouTube videos. They usually make money due to the ads that run during their videos but some make money through the numbers of viewers.

Many RVers have created a money-making YouTube channel by simply being themselves. To make your own YouTube channel, you will need Wi-Fi, a computer, and a way to record yourself. You can then create your channel, whether it's about your life as a full-time RVer or focusing on a talent you have, such as painting. For instance, you could create videos where you are giving classes on how to start painting.

There are no general requirements for creating your YouTube channel, other than the supplies you need, an idea, and then reading YouTube's guidelines.

To help you start out, I have a bonus for you. Get the 'Youtube Celebrity' video course for FREE. This course will take you step-by-step through making a successful YouTube channel and help you gain subscribers on YouTube.

All you have to do is go to this link, **http://eepurl.com/ggIwmD**, and enter your name and e-mail ID.

By signing up for this course you will also be signing up for my e-mail list, to which I send e-mails with bonus RV living tips and content.

Bibliography

Amazondelivers.jobs. (2019). Amazon CamperForce. [online] Available at: http://www.amazondelivers.jobs/about/camperforce/.

Anon, (n.d.). Full Time RV Living Planning -. [online] Available at: https://yourfulltimervliving.com/full-time-rv-living/full-time-rv-living-planning.

Buemi, Megan. "Why Retiring To An RV Is The Way To Go". Rvshare.Com, https://rvshare.com/blog/retiring-to-rv/.

Bunis, D. (n.d.). Learn How to Choose the Right Medigap Plan. [online] AARP. Available at: https://www.aarp.org/health/medicare-insurance/info-2017/choosing-right-medigap-plan.html.

Camphost.org. (n.d.). What Is A Camp Host? | Camp Host Jobs. [online] Available at: http://www.camphost.org/what-is-a-camp-host/.

Doman, E. (2015). 7 Popular Types of RVs & Motorhomes: Pros vs. Cons. [online] Compact Appliance. Available at:

https://learn.compactappliance.com/types-of-rvs-and-motorhomes/.

Explore.va.gov. (n.d.). Apply for Health Care | Explore VA Benefits. [online] Available at: https://explore.va.gov/health-care.

Henkel, Stephanie. (2019). "Full-Time RVing: How To Downsize Your Home To An RV". Axleaddict. Available at: https://axleaddict.com/rvs/Full-Time-RVing-Downsize-Your-Home.

Levin, H. (n.d.). How to Prepare for Full-Time RV Living: Tips & Checklist. [online] Moneycrashers.com. Available at: https://www.moneycrashers.com/prepare-living-rv-full-time-tips-checklist/.

Medicare.gov. (n.d.). How to compare Medigap policies | Medicare. [online] Available at: https://www.medicare.gov/supplements-other-insurance/how-to-compare-medigap-policies.

Medicare.gov. (2015). What's a Medicare Advantage Plan?. [online] Available at: https://www.medicare.gov/pubs/pdf/11474.pdf.

Payne, Howard, and Linda Payne. "Our 2010 Budget By Month". RV-Dreams, https://www.rv-dreams.com/2010-Budget.html..

Popp, M. (2019). 15 Tips for Getting the Best Price on an RV or Camper. [online] TripSavvy. Available at: https://www.tripsavvy.com/get-the-best-price-on-an-rv-or-camper-4159570.

"RV Memberships: Which Should You Join? - Follow Your Detour". Follow Your Detour, https://www.followyourdetour.com/rv-memberships/.

RVing Guide. (n.d.). How Do Full Time RVers Handle Health Care And Medical Issues? | The RVing Guide. [online] Available at: https://rv-roadtrips.thefuntimesguide.com/rv_medical/.

Rogers, J. (2019). RVer Jobs on the Road - Your RV Lifestyle. [online] Your RV Lifestyle. Available at: https://www.your-rv-lifestyle.com/rver-jobs/.

Rosenberg, Eric. "The 8 Best Expense Tracker Apps To Use In 2019". The Balance, 2018, https://www.thebalance.com/best-expense-tracker-apps-4158958.

Swartz, N. (2014). How to Choose the Right RV to Live in (for Full-time Travelers). [online] Wand'rly Magazine. Available at:

https://wandrlymagazine.com/article/complete-guide-to-buying-rvs/.

"Tips For Saving Money While Living Full-Time In An RV - Follow Your Detour". Follow Your Detour, https://www.followyourdetour.com/saving-money-while-full-time-rving/.

TripSavvy. (n.d.). How to Travel With Prescription Drugs. [online] Available at: https://www.tripsavvy.com/tips-for-traveling-with-prescription-drugs-2972759.

Quibell, C. (n.d.). What happens if you want to go full-time and your spouse doesn't? - Roaming RV. [online] Roaming RV. Available at: http://roamingrv.com/full-time-rving-3/.

Leave a Review?

Throughout the process of writing this book, I have tried to put down as much value and knowledge for the reader as possible. Some things I knew some others I spent the time to research. I hope you found this book to be of benefit to you.

If you liked the book, would you consider **leaving a review** for it on Amazon? It would really help my book, and I would be grateful to you for letting other people know that you like it.

Yours Sincerely,

George Lee